END OF WATCH

The Terry Melancon Jr. Story

by

Vicki Melancon

Bloomington, IN  Milton Keynes, UK

AuthorHouse™
1663 Liberty Drive, Suite 200
Bloomington, IN 47403
www.authorhouse.com
Phone: 1-800-839-8640

AuthorHouse™ *UK Ltd.*
500 Avebury Boulevard
Central Milton Keynes, MK9 2BE
www.authorhouse.co.uk
Phone: 08001974150

© 2007 Vicki Melancon. All rights reserved.

No part of this book may be reproduced, stored in a retrieval system, or transmitted by any means without the written permission of the author.

First published by AuthorHouse 4/10/2007

ISBN: 978-1-4259-9647-5 (sc)

Printed in the United States of America
Bloomington, Indiana

This book is printed on acid-free paper.

Cover design by Jeremy Monroe
www.endofwatch.org

This book is dedicated to Kaylan, Lacey, Craig, Grace, Amelia, the Baton Rouge Police Department, Healing Place Church, and mostly to my husband, Terry, whose love and support made this book possible.

1

As I walked into the office, I looked uneasily at the sky and wondered how long the rain would hold off.

"Hey, Gloria. What's the weather going to be like," I asked our office receptionist.

"Don't know," she said, for a change. "Check the website in the newspaper. It's normally listed on the front page."

Gloria was the person we all went to for any information about weather, current events and the like. If a storm was brewing in our future, we could always count on Gloria for updates and warnings. She was particularly fond of hurricanes. The mapping of an approaching storm was her area of expertise, and we depended on her for the latest updates, which were posted in the reception area for all to see.

Gloria, "G-Lo," as most of us called her, was the matriarch of the office.

August 10, 2005, was busy, and I'd had meetings with clients and a luncheon that had taken up way too much of my time. Sometimes these luncheons were excruciating. If I never eat another piece of chicken breast with an unidentifiable sauce on top, along with new potatoes and string beans, and of course bread pudding for dessert, it will be fine with me.

I am the marketing representative for a large title insurance company in Baton Rouge. On this particular day, I had spent much of my time outside of the office, but had hurried back before five o'clock to check messages and plan for the next day.

This was my quiet time—the time spent checking on files and sitting in front of my computer inputting information about clients and contacts that I had visited.

The weather was always important to me in planning for the next day. A rainy day could mean that my agenda may have to be changed. In South Louisiana, weather changes drastically from day to day, even from hour to hour. When we have rain, it floods city streets. And in August, afternoon thunderstorms happen almost daily.

I went to the website Gloria had suggested to get my weather update, and I was shocked at what I saw in bold headlines printed across the site:

Policemen Shot. One Dead, Two Wounded. Details to Follow.

Oh no, I thought. *Our city has not had a policeman killed in a few years.*

My son, Terry Lee Melancon, Jr., was a narcotics detective for the city of Baton Rouge. He absolutely loved his job. Terry had been trained by the best in the police force, and he was always prepared to protect our community every day that he went out on the street.

He had followed in the footsteps of his grandfather and his uncle, both of whom had served in law enforcement, and I knew that Terry was doing what he loved to do. I think most policemen do the job because they love it. They could not put themselves between crime and society for any other reason.

A policeman dead.

My mind started to race. There was no way that could be my son. Surely with more than six hundred policemen on the force, the odds were slim that it would be my son.

Information like this is numbing for anyone who loves a police officer. I think I went into some kind of auto mode and told myself that it was silly to think that it could be Terry. I had to stop my mind from wandering to the point of panic. I could feel my blood pressure rising, and I started to get flushed. It became difficult to breath, and I heard myself gasping for air. The more I dwelled on the words on the computer screen, the worse I felt.

Calm down. Think. What should I do?

Calling the police department would be like calling the school when your children were young just to see if they were all right. I had always been an overprotective mother, and now I felt a little like I had when Terry was young. I just need to call and check. I rehearsed the conversation that I was going to have with the person on the phone, as I was reassured that the fallen officer was not my son. I felt that it would be a bit awkward, but I didn't care. I decided to make that call.

I knew that if Terry found out, he would make fun of me and probably get a good laugh out of it. Nonetheless, I decided I would get the news I wanted and would worry about the repercussions later. The jokes would probably come up at every social event for the next few months. I could already hear them. "Terry's mom always calls to make sure he's okay. Go, mom. Are you going to pack his lunch and make sure he takes his vitamins, too?" But the longer I waited, the more my heart raced. Calling was something I needed to do.

I decided to dial his cell phone first. It rang and rang, then went to voice mail.

I dialed again.

Voice mail again.

I thought that he was probably at the scene of the crime, looking for whoever had killed and hurt his buddies and that he simply didn't have time to answer. At times when I had called him before, if Terry was too busy to talk, he would just call me back later. He was an undercover narcotics detective and spent many hours on stakeouts waiting for drug deals to go down. He often called during these times.

Just answer your phone, T.

I called again, praying that it would not go to voice mail.

Just answer the phone.

He would sometimes answer quickly and say, "Can't talk. Gotta go." This meant that he was busy and that he would call me back when he got a minute. Being a family member of a police officer was difficult, and Terry respected that. He knew it was important to us to be able to stay in touch with him and to hear from him regularly. He tried his best to answer our calls. But because he was so busy, he would often cut us off with a short but sweet "not a good time to talk" conversation. This time I really wanted to hear the sound of his voice.

Dialing felt strange to me. I tried to convince myself that I was overreacting as I am prone to do on occasion, much to the amusement of my family. As I continued dialing his number, I played the conservation over in my mind that Terry would surely have with me.

"Yeah Mom. I'm fine, but I gotta go. Bye."

I dialed again and again and got his voice mail every time. This had happened before, but this time a sick feeling came over me.

Okay. Calm down and think. Who do I call? Where do I look up the number?

I was fumbling for a number, any number, when my daughter, Lacey, called.

We spoke several times during most days, but when she heard the tremor in my voice she said, "What's wrong?" I told her about what I'd read on the website and that I was looking up the number for the police department just to get more information. She calmed me down a little by assuring me that it probably wasn't " T," our nickname for Terry. Finally, I found the number to the police department and dialed it.

A sergeant answered, and I told him who I was. I told him that I knew that this call may seem strange, but I just wanted to know if my son was okay. I told him that I had read about a shooting, and that I didn't need to know anything other than if my son was fine.

Just tell me those words, please.

His voice gave him away.

"We don't know much about the incident as it just happened, but I do know that it was someone in your son's division. It was a plain-clothed officer, and it was definitely the narcotics division."

I knew that there were only a handful of officers in Terry's division and that whoever it was, I was likely to know him. I started to pray, prayers that I could only repeat over and over again.

Help me, God. Please help me.

"Where can I reach you, Mrs. Melancon?" the sergeant said. "I will call you back in five minutes."

I could feel panic rising in me and I could not recite a number to him. I didn't know my number.

Several of my co-workers heard the panic in my voice and surrounded my desk. I looked at one of them and asked for my office number. I could not think. They took over, trying to console me while they gave the sergeant the number.

I could feel those five minutes passing by one second at a time, then another and then another. I ticked them off in my head.

I could not take my eyes off of that phone. It held all of the power over my life. Everything could change drastically with just one ring. My world could come crashing down. My mind became blank. Dark.

It was like a tunnel vision effect around me as I focused on the call I was about to receive.

I thought about Lacey, waiting by her phone, waiting for me to tell her everything was fine.

I jumped when the phone finally rang and unsteadily picked up the receiver. I held my breath as I listened.

2

"Mrs. Melancon, I need to tell you that Terry was shot, but he is okay. Someone is with him. He was shot in the leg, and I assure you that he is going to be okay. Two other officers were shot as well. Where are you now? Chief LeDuff wants to pick you up and bring you to the hospital."

The blood rushed from my face. I could not say anything. I handed the phone to my co-worker, and she gave him directions.

This can't be. I guess if you were shot in the leg, at least your chances of survival are good. How bad could it be?

I wondered if he was in pain.

Please, God, take care of him until we get there.

What do I need to do? I have to call my husband. Where did he say he was going this morning?

As an equipment salesman, Terry Sr. sometimes drives up to three hours away on any given day. I prayed that he was home. With trembling fingers, I dialed his number, sending up a silent prayer of thanks when he answered.

"T's been shot," I exclaimed. "It's only in the leg. They've assured me he'll be fine. He's at the Baton Rouge General Hospital, and I will be on my way there."

"I'm on my way," Terry Sr. responded. I could hear the fear in his voice.

"I'll meet you there."

"Have you called Kaylan? Where is she?"

"I think she's working."

Kaylan is our youngest daughter and was twenty-two years old at the time. She and Terry were close—almost had a parent-daughter relationship. He adored her and showed it by joking and picking on her most of her life. She looked up to him and valued his "boyfriend" advice most of the time. Terry's idea of boyfriend advice was that all her boyfriends were thugs and losers and that she just didn't need to date. "Just hang out with me," was his response when she was between boyfriends.

Kaylan's life was very busy. She attended LSU and worked at a local cell phone store as a sales person. She was good at what she did. She could tell you all of the differences between the phones and programs that were offered in her store. One thing about working in a cell phone store, you are usually the first to get a new phone or to demo a new one that's just about to be released. So when the slightest thing would go wrong with her phone, she was excited to go to the next one. It was almost like getting a new toy for her.

That day she was having trouble with her phone. She had decided to cancel her old one and had started to transfer her information to her new phone. Kaylan was the guru of data retrieval. If anyone in the store had problems transferring their data, Kaylan was the one her peers would call. She could transfer data from a phone that was on life support. She knew exactly what computer program would work if nothing else did. She had never had a problem doing this task, but today was different.

She hooked her phone up to the computer to start the process, but it was denied. She tried again and again and was denied repeatedly. This had never happened before. She became very frustrated.

While she was working on the problem, one of her co-workers was helping a city policeman with his phone. A large radio was attached to his belt along with his gun. In a loud radio screech, she heard a young woman's voice practically yelling, "Officer down. I repeat, officer down."

Both the policeman and Kaylan's co-worker were visibly disturbed. Kaylan noticed the frightened expressions on their faces, but did not become concerned herself. It didn't seem possible that it could be her precious brother who she loved so much. Not her Terry.

While she was still working on the problem with her phone, I called her. She debated whether to answer because that would disconnect her from the computer.

We usually spoke several times a day, and often my call would to go to voice mail, which meant she was with a customer. She would always finish helping the customer and then return my call. Very seldom did I get Kaylan to answer. I called and prayed.

Answer. Please answer, Kaylan. God, please get her to answer.

"Hey Mom. What's up?"

Trying my best to defuse the situation, I choked and said the words.

"Terry's been shot."

The words seemed unreal. I assured her that he was only shot in the leg, but told her that she needed to go to the hospital right away.

Kaylan paced the floor of her store, totally shocked. She could not think of what her next move should be. She simply went blank.

Her boss approached her and calmed her down before he gave her directions on how to get to the hospital. On the way, she unknowingly drove past the street where the shootings occurred and wondered what had happened that would cause so many police to gather in one area. When she arrived at the hospital, she wondered why so many police cars were lined up outside. She never thought that her brother was the reason. She could never have imagined what she was about to encounter.

When Kaylan approached the hospital, she asked the policeman directing traffic where she could park. He shrugged his shoulders

"Lady, there's so much going on right now, just park wherever you can find a spot."

Apparently there were a large number of reporters trying to get to the hospital, and the policeman thought that Kaylan was with the media.

She told him that she was Terry's sister, and he immediately flagged her into a handicapped parking lot in front of the emergency room door. That seemed a bit strange to her. It still did not occur to her that this was all about her brother. She wondered what was going on.

Kaylan was a bit confused as she tried to sort through her feelings of anxiety.

Just the day before, Terry had been hounding her about renewing her six-month overdue inspection sticker. They talked most days. Kaylan would call him as she walked from class to class. Every day he would ask her, "Did you get it renewed yet?" Her answer was always "Not today, but I promise I will."

Being a sympathetic mom, I would sometimes feel sorry for my little girl because she worked so hard and had so much to do between school and work, but Terry was persistent about renewing that sticker. One day he called her to chat and asked again if she had taken care of the sticker. She was so tired of telling him no that she fibbed just a little and told him that she had.

"Are you sure?" he said.

"Yes, Terry, I did."

"You're sure, right?"

"What's up, T?"

"Look in your rear view mirror."

She glanced up to find Terry behind her, waving from his car.

She had been busted.

"Now let's go get that sticker," Terry said.

Kaylan was the youngest in our family, and to us she was still our baby. She was ten years younger than Terry, and although she was in her twenties, Terry treated her like she was still in high school, scrutinizing her dates and giving her advice that she chose to ignore for the most part. But Kaylan adored her brother.

I felt blessed to be able to say that my children were best friends with each other. It always warmed my heart to see them spend so much time together, to know they did so because they wanted to.

As I waited for the police car to come and take me to the hospital, my thoughts turned to Lacey. Lacey was a stay-at-home mom to Grace and Amelia, who were only eleven months apart, and I knew that she would have to pack them up for the trip to the hospital. Packing up a two-year-old and a three-year-old to go anywhere was always a chore. I knew that when the time came to tell her what had happened to Terry, she would be very upset, too upset to gather the children and drive to the hospital. That time had come, and I knew I had to tell her.

"Lacey, Terry's been shot in the leg. They said he'll be okay, but you'll need to come to the hospital."

I heard her gasp, and then she began to cry. My heart hurt for my girls. I wanted to be there in person to tell them and hold them, but there was no time. As a mother, the hurt your children experience becomes your hurt as well.

I'm sure God was looking out for Lacey because just minutes after she learned the news, my sister and her two boys, who were visiting from California, arrived at her home in time to baby-sit the girls.

I knew I had to get to that hospital. The police chief had not arrived, but I could no longer sit and wait. I wanted to see Terry. My boss and several co-workers who had waited with me said, "Let's go."

I needed to be moving forward. The waiting was torture.

We drove recklessly, breaking every speed limit and running yellow lights. On our way, my boss said, "Let's say a prayer." He prayed that everything would be okay. He asked God to help us remember that He was in control. To this day, I thank God that I had a boss who was a caring and prayerful friend.

My anxiety level raised another notch as we approached a traffic jam. It slowly dawned on me that we were at the location where the shooting had taken place. Swarms of policemen were walking around, some with tablets in their hands, some talking in groups, some wearing plain clothes. All looked very solemn. I felt a chill. I knew that something was gravely wrong.

There was tape surrounding the street, and a tent covered the area. The traffic jam had stopped four lanes of traffic. As we slowed down, the hunched-over shoulders of the police told me that I had good reason to be so afraid.

Finally, we inched our way to within a block of the hospital. Again, there were hundreds of police. The hospital was literally unapproachable.

My boss yelled to an officer that I was the mother of one of the policeman who had been shot, and they quickly lifted the barricade to let us through.

I was rushed by a half-dozen policemen to a room just inside the emergency room entrance. Probably another dozen people were in this room. It was obvious that they knew something that I didn't know.

Waiting in the hospital that day could only be described as surreal. *Why isn't anyone coming in to tell me that he is fine?*

"It can't be that bad, right?" I said over and over.

When my husband arrived, we held each other more tightly than we ever had before. More people were entering and leaving the room, but I couldn't talk. All I could do was reach out to God.

Help me. Please help me.

The news traveled fast throughout the city. I am certain that many people knew what had happened to Terry before we did.

It occurred to me as I waited that you can see the spirit of God in perfect strangers. I desperately looked into the eyes of some of the people in that room, and I was drawn to a man who was somehow holding my hand. Although I had never met this man before, our spirits spoke. I knew that he was a man of God and that he would be able to comfort me in a way that God knew I needed. I softly said that I needed him to pray. He gently prayed and kept reassuring me that God was in control. "Keep focusing on Jesus. God is here. Everything will be okay."

Lacey and Kaylan arrived at the same time. We hugged, and then we just sat there, all of us anxious, all of us more afraid than we had ever been. The fear on the faces of my family was difficult to bear. I wanted to tell them good news. But I had no news. I was beginning to realize that maybe this would be worse than we had been told. We held each other and asked God to give us strength.

Finally, Chief LeDuff made his way into the room with Mayor Melvin "Kip" Holden and several police officers. One walked over to me, another to my husband. One to Lacey. One to Kaylan. My hands began to tremble.

Chief LeDuff bent down in front of me and took my hands in his.

"He's gone," he said. "I'm so sorry. He's gone."

3

IN 1974, HOSPITALS WERE very different from what they are today. As I lay squirming in a steel-rimmed bed in a stark, sterile room, I watched the large clock attached to the wall at the foot of the bed. Being in labor for more than twelve hours, my focus stayed on the second hand of that clock, ticking…ticking…ticking, every second accentuating my pain as I wondered how long it would take for my child to be born. My husband, Terry, sat in a cheap naugahyde chair at the side of my bed.

"I can't believe how slowly time is going by. This chair is so uncomfortable. I wish it would recline," Terry complained. He was as nervous as I was and becoming irritable.

"You're uncomfortable?" I couldn't believe he had said that. "Try trading places with me. I'm stuck between labor pains and pain medicine that hasn't kicked in yet. But, that's nothing, I guess. *You* can't recline, that *must* really be a hardship for you. How can you possibly stand it?" I shot back at him.

As another pain raced through my body, I forgot that this was the man I loved. All I knew was that I hurt and he was partly responsible. As the contraction eased, I noticed the contrite look on his face and felt badly for having been cross with him, but only for a moment. Another contraction was coming.

At twenty years old, my husband and I were expecting our first child. In the early seventies, the technology to determine the sex of a child was not available for women scheduled to have a routine birth. The sonogram machine was only used for high-risk patients, so we were not blessed to know what the sex of our unborn child would be. Terry and I simply went to the hospital with a boy name and girl name in mind, and finally after more than twelve hours of hard labor, we had our first child whom we named after his father.

Terry Jr. arrived a few weeks early and weighed only five-and-a-half pounds. His little digestive system was a bit premature, and suddenly I was a mother trying to ease the pain of colic and a bad reaction to the formula I'd fed him.

Many years later, Terry continued to have trouble with spicy foods. He always attributed his digestive problems to the fact that he was premature. I'm not convinced of that, but Terry's answer for any ailment he ever suffered was to say that he was premature. Hangnails were a product of being premature, the way he saw it.

Once Terry passed the formula and colicky stage, he was a delight. I could not believe this precious baby was mine. My world was complete. I had a husband I loved and a son to care for. Life was good. I had always wanted to be a mother, and I took the job very seriously.

We lived in a neighborhood in Baton Rouge where most of the couples were students. All of the wives were all very young women who had kids and depended on each other for valuable advice. One neighbor, Versa Stickel, was a little older than I, and we instantly became fast friends. She was married to a biology professor at LSU and loved being a mom to their two daughters, Sarah and Martha. Martha was Terry's age. Versa taught me how to make fresh bread, how to sew and how to make fresh baby food. It was fun learning how to take care of my baby. That was my most important goal, to be a great mom.

I was brought up in a strict Catholic family, and the discipline I learned in my childhood was very valuable to me. We went to church every Sunday, come rain or shine. My parents were excellent role models, and we were a typical Catholic family. I was the oldest of six children, with all of us being born within a ten-year span. My mom stayed home to take care of us while my dad worked hard to provide us with a lifestyle that was probably above middle class. Our needs were always met, and we never had to worry about anything. I wanted to give my child an upbringing like that, to teach him strong values, to help him become a strong and good man.

My siblings and I attended Catholic schools, which had served to reinforce the discipline of being committed to the church. I will admit that at that time attending church was a duty for me, and I was not as committed to God as I would become later. I was more committed to the church. But I knew that God was someone I should go to during the times in my life when I needed comfort. Instead of going to Him for everything, my approach was almost like a last-ditch effort. As happens with many people, circumstances would occur later in my life that would show me a different way. I now know that God puts circumstances in our lives in order for our opportunities to grow. These are the moments when God shows us His power and his ability to comfort and heal.

I feel that I am very fortunate to have been brought up with the Christian morals and values that my parents instilled in me. It was always church on Sunday, followed by a visit to Piccadilly, a buffet style diner that suited all eight of our tastes, which was the perfect solution for Sunday dinner in my dad's eyes. This tradition was so rich throughout my childhood that I made sure that my new family followed it as best we could.

As young parents, our budget was tight. We stayed at home and learned to have fun with the simple things. Terry Sr. and I would sit on the steps of our small house and watch young Terry ride up and down the driveway with his big wheel. He was so agile that at the end of the driveway he would cut his wheel into a spin that would send the bike into a whirling circular motion. Terry was always the child that could outride most of the kids in our neighborhood, although to be fair, most of them were girls.

We lived in a small wood-framed two-bedroom house built in the 1950s. Today, it would be considered a cozy cottage, but, in fact, it was in need of a few too many repairs for us to bother with. Terry was an outside, backyard, tough kid. He loved playing in his yard. His dad built a clubhouse in the back that became his fort. A tire swing hung from a huge old oak tree centered in the middle of the back yard. The tree was so old that grass refused to grow under the shaded area. Terry turned this area into a big city where he could use all of his dump trucks and cars that he loved to collect. The backyard was the envy of his friends, and most of the time they were right there playing with him.

Lacey was born when Terry turned three. He loved her so much that I had to watch him closely because several times I had found him sitting in her crib trying to hold her. And as they got a few years older, space in our little home became very tight. We found a three-bedroom house in my aunt's neighborhood that was a few years old and moved across the street from her. Within a three-block area there were dozens of kids, most about the same age of ours. Woods bordered a field located behind our neighbor's home. This became the kids' ball field, clubhouse and anything else that their imaginations would allow them to dream.

Aunt Faye, who was my mom's younger sister and her husband, Uncle Jay, were always two of my favorite people. Their two boys, Chris and Scott, were a bit older that my children, but their daughter, Bridget, was Lacey's age. They were inseparable. During the summer months, Lacey was always at Bridget's or Bridget was at our house. However, Lacey was very shy and when she started elementary school, she found it difficult to make friends. She would come home from school and cry because she had no one to play with at recess. But at home, she was a star. Terry made sure of it.

When the neighborhood kids got together to play baseball, kickball or hide and seek, Terry always made sure that Lacey was the first to get picked. Her big brother always made her feel special. Terry wouldn't let anything happen to her. Her haven was her neighborhood, although school became torture for her.

The girls in her class were cruel as young girls can be. They seemed to hang out together in packs, and if you were included you were cool; otherwise you were an outsider. They reveled in excluding the un-cool girls and made fun of them. Lacey was considered very un-cool.

Terry and Lacey went to a private school. It stretched our budget, but it was a priority for us. Most of the children who attended this school were from affluent families and wore the best designer clothes. We could not afford those things as well as a good education for our children. This was the final straw for Lacey. Not only was she an outsider, but she couldn't wear the cool clothes that the other children wore. That weighed heavily on her. As a parent, I found nothing wrong with the less expensive look-alikes of the name brands, but Lacey knew the difference.

I tried hard to teach both of my children what really matters in life. "Popularity can vanish in a moment," I said. I told them that popularity seems to always have an entourage, people who will do anything to be included. You can't judge someone by what they wear. There are much more important things in life. I told them that they should always remember that Jesus was by their side, that he didn't judge by what people wore. I said that He always knew what to do and where to go for answers, that it is much more important to be someone God would be proud of. I taught them that you make a lasting impression on someone by the good things you do. Then and only then will people remember you as being someone special. And Terry and Lacey were special.

My life revolved around my children. Being able to stay home with them was very rewarding. As Terry grew, he and I developed a close relationship. He became very attached to me, so much so that in his first year of kindergarten, he had such a difficult time adjusting to being away from me that he'd had to repeat the grade. He would later tell everyone that he had failed kindergarten because he didn't want to leave his mom, but he was born in January and was young for his class. At least that's the excuse I gave myself when it was suggested that he stay back. That sounded much better than having to admit that my child failed kindergarten.

I volunteered for everything at his school. I was a room mother. I went on field trips and helped with any other projects that I could. I don't know if this helped or hurt Terry, but as time went by, he and I realized that school was a necessary evil that we would work through together. I assured him that both of us would survive.

4

SURVIVAL SEEMED A LITTLE bit easier by the time Kaylan came along. She was ten years younger than Terry. I can still remember telling Terry and Lacey that I was pregnant, and their reaction was that of two children who had just received the best Christmas gift possible. She was even better than the puppy they had received the Christmas before.

Kaylan was a perfect baby. She came home to four parents, Terry Sr. and I and Lacey and Terry. The only problem with Kaylan was that she slept all the time. Lacey and Terry always wanted to play with her, and they did everything they could think of to awaken her. When she would finally wake up, Terry would get on the floor with her and make her laugh uncontrollably. Kaylan was his baby.

After the third child, the disciplined mothering that I had enforced with Terry and Lacey became somewhat more relaxed. It didn't bother me as much when she got dirty. I reasoned that surely dirt was healthy in some way. I figured that was a good way to build up the body's immune system. Instead of rushing home to make sure afternoon naps were strategically enforced, which is what I had done with Lacey and Terry, Kaylan was lucky if she got a nap on the way to one of the kids' ball practices or dance lessons. Nevertheless, Kaylan was a good baby and adapted well to our crazy schedule.

When Terry was in his early teens, I allowed him to watch Kaylan on occasion. This was very seldom, and usually only when I had exhausted all other babysitting options. Because he loved playing with her, whatever Kaylan wanted to do, Terry would do it. This was fine when I was at home because I could monitor their activities and quickly abort the ones that were not acceptable. But when Terry babysat, his way of appeasing Kaylan was to let her have her way. It kept her quiet. A perfect solution.

While babysitting one day, Kaylan asked him to put her in a sleeping bag and hang her on the frame of the bedroom door. He admitted later that he had quite a time hanging it, especially since she was about four years old and weighed more than thirty pounds. But Terry worked hard at this task and finally attached the sleeping bag string to the top between the hinge and the door.

They laughed and giggled until she was ready to get down. The problem was that he was not big enough to lift the sleeping bag up over the hinge to loosen it from the doorframe. The giggles stopped abruptly.

Terry knew that if he called me, there would be trouble. His dad was at work, and they were not to call him unless blood or fire was involved. When I arrived home, Terry had a terrified look on his face as he tried to tell me what had happened. Thank God I had gotten home early. I could hear a muffled voice from the sleeping bag attached to the doorframe still housing my daughter. I put a chair under her, lifting her high enough that I could remove the bag.

She emerged with her hair matted with sweat and her cheeks glowing red from the well-insulated sleeping bag. She was so excited to be out, and when she saw Terry they both laughed so much that it was hard to fuss at either of them.

I don't think that Terry ever realized that he was doing anything wrong. He was making his little sister happy. That was what he did. In return, Kaylan looked up to Terry. He was a great role model for her, and she wanted to be like her big brother.

As she grew older, Kaylan's gentle heart more and more apparent. She never had a problem attracting friends because she loved pleasing people and enjoyed helping others. She always put forth her best effort no matter what she did. Kaylan was an achiever. In high school, she was voted student body president, and one year, she earned the distinction of being voted Student of the Year.

Kaylan was a gifted child, and we were best friends. She loved her mama and often wrote sweet poems expressing her feelings. She wrote beautiful poetry, and I was delighted when several of her works were published.

Her brother became her staunch protector, sometimes to Kaylan's distress. First dates, homecoming dances, the movies, all became torture for her. She knew that she had to bring her date home to meet her parents *and* Terry. She would usually spend the entire afternoon preparing for her big night out. It seemed that Terry always found out when she was going to leave because he would show up with one or more of his friends to drill the unsuspecting date. They would stand in the kitchen knowing that the boy would have to walk past them. They would fold their arms while glaring, and then begin the inquisition until Kaylan would rush out to save the poor boy.

This procedure had been perfected when Lacey was in high school, and Terry was not going to let anything happen to either of his sisters. Although he had a reputation for being a nice guy, the girls' dates knew that they had better treat Terry's sisters with respect and dignity.

Terry was one of the oldest kids in the neighborhood, and if he said that everyone should play hide and seek, then that was the way it was. He always chose who had to be "it." Of course, Terry was never "it," and he was so fast that he was hardly ever caught. But this was the unspoken rule of the neighborhood. The kids knew the chain of command and abided by this unspoken rule. Terry gave directions, and they followed his lead.

Every neighborhood has a "Little Al," someone who can usually be talked into anything. It was also understood that Al would be the first one to be "it" because he could never catch anyone. No one wanted to be the one chasing the other kids. That was the worst position on the team. But in order for Al to play, he had to be "it" first. Al would play long enough to get frustrated and then run home to his dad.

All of the other kids knew it was time for them to run, too.

Al's running home!

That was what the kids dreaded—Al's dad, Big Al, coming out looking for the dirty little scoundrels who had made his boy cry.

The street would become as empty as if it were the middle of the night with all of the kids safely hiding until Big Al went back inside.

Big Al did his best to take up for his son, but he knew that his son was always getting in trouble. He also knew that if Al came home crying, it was because Al had refused to be "it" once again, and since he could never catch anyone he could not relinquish this position to anyone else.

Al's dad would come looking for the gang to give them the "talk" about including his son in the games and order everyone to stop making him cry. The fact is that Al cried so often that his tears no longer worked on the gang.

I remember one day Al and Terry were playing when Al decided to build a campfire in the field in the middle of summer when we had not had rain for some time. Needless to say, within minutes the fire was raging, and the fire department had to be called.

When Terry and Al were a little older, just after Al had gotten his driver's license, he decided to take his boat out to the river to try out his new motor and asked Terry to go along. He forgot to mention that his dad had instructed him not to take the boat out under any circumstance because the motor was still in the box and had to be properly attached. A minor detail in Little Al's book. He figured that attaching a motor couldn't be that hard.

"Hey Terry, help me take this motor out of the box," he said.

"You sure your dad wants us to do this, Al?" Terry wasn't sure about this.

"Yeah, sure, he won't mind, and we'll be home long before he gets home from work. Let's just take it to the river and see what it will do."

Terry still wasn't sure. "I've never attached a boat motor. Have you?"

"It can't be that hard," Al responded impatiently.

"There sure are a lot of extra bolts left here," Terry said after they had bolted a few, and Al had announced that they were finished. "That can't be good."

"They always give you extras. That's just extras," Al reassured him.

The boys went to the boat launch and pushed it slowly into the middle of the river. Instead of starting the motor at the launch, they decided that pushing the boat into the water would give them more room to see what it could do.

With one quick pull of the starter pulley, the motor rattled and shook a bit but finally started with the propeller spinning frantically and a puff of smoke rising from the motor. The boys watched in horror as it started to wobble from the frame of the boat.

"Terry!" Al screamed. "What do we do? We need to kill the engine. It's coming loose."

"I don't know. How do you stop it?"

"My dad said that there's a kill switch somewhere, but I don't remember where it is."

The motor separated from the frame of the boat, rolled to one side and sputtered, then slightly turned, looking like a fish flopping in the water. With the propeller still going, the boys watched it sink to the bottom of the river.

Al's father was not happy when he found out about the incident, and we didn't see Al for a while. But Al grew up to be a fine young man. He is a policeman, and as adults, he and Terry often laughed about the crazy things that they had done.

Although Terry always had a lot of friends with whom to do things, more than anyone else, he loved to hang out with his dad. They were best friends. Terry depended on him for advice, and Terry Sr. had a way of telling it like it was. He spoke only truth to Terry.

Those two were sometimes inseparable and spent every winter throughout Terry's childhood hunting for anything and everything. They changed their prey with the seasons.

Usually after a long day of hunting, all of the men would gather around a campfire to have a few beers and talk about their day—who had shot the biggest what and so forth. As the night wore on, the men would get louder and louder, and the conversations would get somewhat become more adult. At this point, Terry Sr., concerned about what his son would hear, always excused himself, and he and Terry would retreat to their camp.

Terry Sr. was always cautious about making sure his son was not exposed to bad language and the occasional drinking that occurred during their hunting trips. He protected Terry as best he could. He made sure that his son knew what was and was not appropriate language.

Terry learned many lessons while hunting, but his greatest was an appreciation of God's beautiful earth. The hunting camp was a wilderness of more than sixty acres with about a dozen trails through which hunters could navigate with four-wheelers. The terrain was hilly and decorated with huge cliffs. The trails usually ran alongside the drop-off points of the cliffs. It was a beautiful setting for father and son to enjoy together.

They began their hunting trips when Terry was about four years old. Throughout this time, my husband neglected to mention that he was letting my son drive the four-wheeler by himself, but Terry told me. I remember becoming very upset. Terry was only five at the time.

"Come on, Vicki. He's a boy. I was standing right there," my husband informed me.

Terry chimed in that he couldn't even reach the bottom peddle, but he could still drive.

"What's the bottom peddle for?" I said

"It's the brakes, but it's not like you need to use them when you're going as slow as Terry does," Terry Sr. replied. He promised me that it wouldn't happen again, although I'm sure it did, and I worried about those two when they were out being boys.

To get to the secluded campground, it was necessary to travel a long stretch of a road that had nothing on it for ten or so miles—no houses, no street lights and you seldom even passed another vehicle.

When Terry was twelve, his dad would allow him to drive his truck along that stretch of road up to the main highway. He could barely touch the accelerator, but he was driving a stick shift. At some point, I realized that there were some things that I just didn't need to know. They only made me worry, and I knew I couldn't stop them from having their fun.

All through junior high and high school, Terry spent all of his weekends with his dad. It was during those times that he learned about being a man. He learned about nature, and he learned to love and appreciate his dad for the lessons he took the time to teach him.

5

In high school, everyone liked Terry. Although he was considered to be one of the cool kids, he made sure to include everyone in his circle of friends, and the girls, especially, were drawn to him. He had no problem getting dates. Once, he even had the dubious honor of his legs being named the "best legs" in the school. A photographer took pictures of the legs of several of the boys and convinced Terry to participate in the competition. The photographs were posted in the cafeteria for judging by the school. Terry won hands down and was soon crowned "Mr. Legs of Woodlawn."

I'm sure he was embarrassed because he neglected to mention this to me. I learned of it at the grocery store when several of his female fans congratulated me on this most honorable award. I went straight home to compliment Terry on his legs.

He said that he really didn't want to hear comments about his legs coming from his mom, but I couldn't resist a joke now and then. And since he always seemed to get into one escapade after another, there was always something to tease him about. Like the time his friend, Tim, got a job delivering flowers at a local florist. When Terry had nothing to do, he would ride with Tim to make deliveries.

Once, they were assigned to bring a sympathy arrangement to a church in the northern part of town. Terry and Tim set about their task, with Terry driving and Tim giving directions.

As they pulled into the church's parking lot, they noticed that a black hearse was parked in front of a long stairwell. A gentlemen dressed in a black suit was standing beside the hearse, looking up at the steep and narrow stairs.

The boys knew what was coming next. The man approached the window of the florist's van and asked if Terry and Tim could help him get the casket up the stairs and into the church.

The boys looked at each other in horror.

"Um, I've never carried a casket before," Terry said. "Are you sure you need our help?"

"Can't you find anyone else to help you?" Tim piped in. "This looks a little creepy to me. I mean, you think the person in that coffin is okay with this?"

"Look guys," the man insisted. "It's just me and you. Come on."

The man walked to the hearse and opened the back to display the dark wooden coffin. He slipped a gurney from the hearse, opened it and started to slide the coffin onto it. He rolled the coffin to the base of the stairs and gave each boy his assignment.

"Terry, you get this bottom left, and Tim can take the bottom right. I will lead up the stairs."

The steps were hard to maneuver because the boys couldn't see their feet to watch where they were going. About midway up, Terry smashed his finger on the rail and dropped his side of the coffin. This created a domino effect with the other two coffin holders.

Almost in slow motion, the coffin slid between Terry and Tim as it began its journey down the stairs. At one point, it began to bounce, and then the lid flew open to reveal an elderly man dressed in a black suit. Finally, it came to rest at the foot of the stairs—now a beat-up coffin holding the body of an elderly man whose ride had caused him to sit up a bit.

Terry and Tim could not get out of there fast enough. They excused themselves and almost ran to the van, neither of them saying a word as they drove back to the florist shop. It was only much later that they could laugh about the incident, but we teased them mercilessly about it.

But Terry had a sweet spirit that you rarely see in young men. He reached out to people and was willing to help whenever he saw the need. I remember one hot August afternoon when he was sitting in our den, which faced the street, and noticed a lady walking past our house with a gas can in her hand. Without thinking or saying a word, he jumped in his truck, picked up the lady and drove her to and from the gas station to fill up her car.

He would help anyone, even those who many high school students wouldn't think to help. One day, I received an envelope in the mail from one of his teachers. I was afraid to open it because I had never had one of his teachers send me a letter. I wondered if his grades were falling or if he had gotten into some kind of trouble. I could only imagine what would be inside. The letter was handwritten and addressed to me:

Mrs. Melancon,

Your son impressed me so much today that I had to take the time and write to you. I was walking down the hall this morning, late for my first class and I had a load of books in my arms. While walking down the hall, passing all the students, I noticed that your son, Terry, was running toward me. He took the books from my arms and walked me to my class, allowing me to catch my breath and enter my classroom.

I want you to know that Terry shows kindness like I rarely see in other students. Terry is a special young man, and I enjoy having him in my class.

Mrs. McNutt

Terry had not mentioned this incident to me, but there was something in his nature that made acts of kindness routine for him. He did it because it was the right thing to do. He did it because he was thoughtful. It made me so proud to know that even when no one was looking he was a wonderful young man. It was like the wristband he wore that read, "WWJD." (What would Jesus do?) He lived by that, and he impressed others with his kindness.

He was equally considerate with his girlfriends. Terry rarely dated for fun. He liked having a steady girlfriend and always chose her carefully. It was important to him that he liked her as well as loved her.

One such girl was Susan, who I actually introduced to him. She was a beautiful girl—tall and thin and blessed with a captivating smile. I was taking a class at LSU with her, and we spent many hours studying together. I knew that she was Terry's type, so I asked her if she wanted to meet my son. I could tell by the way she said "yeah" that she was less than enthusiastic about meeting him. I know she thought Terry probably had a hard time getting dates and that his poor mother was trying her best to fix up her nerdish dork of a son on a date. But I knew that she would like him as much as he would like her.

She agreed to meet him for coffee, and they really hit it off. Terry couldn't thank me enough, and they started dating.

When Terry met Susan, she was living with a wealthy family, working as a nanny to their three children. Her family was scattered, and she rarely spoke to them. I have never understood how a mother and father could cut ties to a sweet girl like her, a girl who was paying her own way through college, especially since she was barely nineteen.

But they had, and she gravitated toward our family, loving the closeness that she hadn't felt in her own family.

Several months after they started dating, the family Susan lived with decided that they wanted a full-time nanny and they told her that she would have to leave. This was devastating news for her, as she had nowhere to go.

Her mother and father ignored her calls. Soon Susan was homeless.

Terry asked his father and me if we would help her, insisting that he would sleep somewhere else while she was in our home. He confided to me that his feelings were changing toward her, but that he knew this was not the right time to tell her. He knew that he had to help her. This situation was way out of my comfort zone, but I knew we needed to help, so I asked her to stay with us until she got back on her feet. She stayed with us for a short while, but she eventually found a friend to help her and moved out.

Once she was okay, Terry told her he didn't think that it would work out between them, but they remained friends. Terry usually remained friends with the girls he dated. That was his way.

One Christmas, Terry Sr. and I were invited to a party with friends that we had known since high school. Phil and Eileen had always been special to us. Eileen and I had grown up in the same neighborhood, and Phil and Terry Sr. were childhood friends as well. But although we had stood in each other's weddings, there were some years that we had not seen each other.

Eileen and Phil had a daughter, Michelle, who had been diagnosed with cancer when she was only four. This disease consumed their lives.

They lived at St. Jude's Children's Hospital for years while Michelle went through different treatments and numerous surgeries. We always kept up with them through mutual friends and phone calls, but visiting was difficult.

When Michelle began to recover and her parents had a little more time to enjoy the normal things in life again, we picked up our friendship right where we had left off.

Since Terry had recently ended his relationship with Susan, we asked him to join us at the party. He knew Eileen and Phil's other children, Renee and Jason, as well as Michelle, and he had often played with them when he was younger. Renee was Terry's age, and Jason was several years younger. Michelle was the youngest.

Jason and Terry were buddies. They were both good-natured and kind, but it had been a few years since they had seen each other. Because they each had grown up in a house full of girls, they could relate to each other. Terry had always liked Renee, too. Growing up, she had been precious with her curly brown hair and hazel eyes. She was a little girly girl.

Several days before the party, Eileen called very upset. She had disturbing news. Renee had just come home from Orlando, and she was pregnant. She had moved there to live with her aunt and to work at Disney World. She had just gotten home and had broken the news. Eileen didn't know what to think or do. Renee was not married, and she refused to disclose the identity of the father. She was doing this alone. Period.

I told Terry Sr. and Terry about Renee's pregnancy just before we went to the party in order to avoid any awkward moments in case the subject came up.

At the party, the adults gathered in one room to rehash old times while Terry, Jason and Renee talked for hours in another. When Jason left to pick his girlfriend, Terry and Renee sat in a corner and talked. Terry called her repeatedly just to hang out over the next few months. He wanted to be a friend she could count on during this time.

Before long, we could tell their friendship was progressing. It did not matter to Terry that she was pregnant with someone else's baby. I could see that he was falling in love with her. I figured that if this was what Terry wanted, then we would love Renee's baby just as we had loved her since she was a baby.

She had a six-pound baby boy whom she named Matthew. Terry was with her in the hospital throughout her labor and delivery. Matthew captured Terry's heart. He just loved that baby. Terry was the only father Matt knew. Terry still lived at home, but often during the night, Renee would call Terry to go to the drug store to pick up medicine for the baby, and Terry would always jump into his car immediately, just as if he were the dad.

I saw a side of Terry that was new and very precious to me. He adored children. He had so much patience with them, especially with Matthew.

Many of Renee and Terry's dates from then on were centered around Matthew. They would go the zoo or the aquarium, with Terry holding Matthew's hand in his and buying him ice cream.

As unconventional as it seemed, it worked.

Terry and Renee dated for another two years before it became obvious to both of them that it wasn't going to work out. Renee felt that she was holding Terry back and decided to stop seeing him.

Terry missed Matthew as much as he did Renee, but he realized that it was for the best. After the break up, he concentrated on his studies and getting out of school.

By this time, he was ready to start a new chapter in his life.

6

Terry's college years zoomed by, and in no time I found myself looking at a young man instead of the boy I had known for so many years. Terry chose to stay at home instead of getting an apartment during the four years he spent at LSU. As he moved into his last semesters, his studies became increasingly difficult. Terry had to study all the time.

I think it just didn't occur to him to move out. He was comfortable and in no hurry to spread his wings. Some of his friends wanted him to share an apartment with them, but he wasn't interested. For us, it was a great arrangement. We loved having him home, and he loved the fact that he didn't have to pay rent and could always count on mama cooking his favorite southern dishes.

"What do you have to eat?" was the first thing he always said when he got home. You could barely get two words out of him before he ate, but after he was full, he would lean back and tell us about his day. We always enjoyed those after-dinner conversations with him. It was about the only time we saw him. Either he was working at the local hardware store or studying. I had no reason to encourage him to move out. The truth was that I was glad he was around.

I realize now that I was fortunate to have spent those extra years with Terry while he went through college. I thank God that it worked out that way. What a precious gift that extra time was. It was even more special to me because Lacey had fallen in love and married, and I was facing the fact that all of my children would soon be gone.

The lessons Lacey learned as a child created an incredible young woman. At first glance, everyone had always noticed her natural beauty. She is small-framed, with large brown eyes and shiny, mahogany brown hair. Her smile is contagious. Yet it's what's inside of Lacey that has always been the most valuable thing about her to me.

She has a passion for life. She loves intently. When I see her with her children, I marvel at the patience and love that she shares with them. She is satisfied with the simple things in life. She rarely shops, except for the necessities, and she is content with herself. And then God blessed her with a wonderful husband. I knew right away that he was made especially for Lacey.

She met Craig when she was working at a restaurant while in college. She was a waitress, and he was her manager. Lacey was attracted to his wonderful smile, not to mention that she thought he was very cute. She had a crush on him, but they were both dating other people at the time. Lacey knew that her relationship with her boyfriend was not working out, but she felt comfortable enough with it to just let it go on as it was. Until she met Craig.

Craig, being the manager, could not date the staff. He felt the same way about his girlfriend as Lacey felt about her boyfriend, but Craig was such a nice guy that he found it difficult to break up with any girl. Because of this, he had devised a system that he felt was foolproof. He would become pitiful, obnoxious, anything that would make the girl run, not walk, away from him, and he worked hard to make them think the breakup was their idea. He would act appropriately sad, but not sad enough to make them feel bad. He just couldn't stand the thought of hurting someone and that way, he could avoid what he hated most in the world—confrontation—and everyone walked away happy.

Lacey found it difficult to approach Craig. It was much easier to have a friendly flirtation. That was safer. But her feelings soon became stronger, and she couldn't deny that there was something special about Craig.

She asked me what she should do. I was uncomfortable giving her advice because I didn't know how Craig felt about her, and I didn't want her to get hurt.

"I think you should pray about this, Lacey. God knows who is best for you, and I feel that He will lead you in the right direction."

Lacey drove to our church, hoping the door would be open. She pulled on the big wooden doors only slightly to peek inside. It was empty. She tugged the door open just enough to allow her to slip in and quietly slid into the last seat. The vastness of the empty church was sobering. She felt that she was alone with God in His house. She hoped she would hear from Him.

Lacey thought about how complicated everything had suddenly become. She had a crush on her boss. He probably didn't even know that she existed, and even it he wanted to date her, he couldn't. He had a girlfriend. She began to pray.

"God, if Craig is someone that You want in my life, please let him call. Otherwise, please take these feelings away from me."

Lacey left the church with a heavy heart.

When she arrived at her apartment, she slowly walked up the stairs to the door. Her roommate, Tracy, was not yet home, so it was just Lacey and Bella, the black and tan cat she had found on the side of the road the year before.

Lacey was always picking up stray cats and dogs and finding homes for them. She once picked up a dog while running in our neighborhood and brought it home. She posted signs all around the area with a picture and her phone number for the owner to call to claim the lost pet. This was a routine for Lacey, and she had mastered the art of finding lost pets their owners.

The owner called and identified the dog. Lacey told her she would return the pet to its home since she was going out. When Lacey pulled up at the address she had been given, she knew that she had made a grave mistake.

The owner lived in the house where Lacey had picked up the dog. The owner was so glad to get her dog back that Lacey decided not to tell her. Her heart had been in the right place.

But that night, it was just Lacey and Bella. The light on the answering machine blinked, and as she stroked Bella, she heard Craig's voice on the machine.

"Hey, Lacey, this is Craig Harrington. I was wondering if you want to go out one day. Call me if you do."

That was a prayer answered very quickly.

Lacey transferred to another restaurant, and she and Craig began to date. Two years later, early one Christmas morning, Craig called to ask us if he could come by and see us. Terry Sr. thought that it was a bit strange, but I knew what was coming. The question. The big question that all guys dread asking the parents of the woman they love.

"May I have your permission to ask your daughter to marry me?" he nervously said.

The answer was easy. "Yes, you have our blessing."

They were engaged and married that same year. It was clear to all of us that Lacey and Craig belonged together.

The thing that Lacey needed most was her brother's approval, and she definitely had that. Terry and Craig were great friends.

Craig and Lacey eventually opened a restaurant of their own in the middle of Baton Rouge's business district. Harrington's Café and Catering is one of the top restaurants in the area. On most days, there is a hungry crowd waiting on the street to get in. Craig and Lacey enjoy talking with and getting to know the people they serve, and many of their patrons have become friends.

The business district is known for the homeless people who wander its streets. Every day, just after the lunch crowd leaves, Craig boxes up dozens of extra lunches for the homeless, who gather daily at the same time for their meal. The boxes are left on the ledge of the restaurant's window, and one by one they come by to get what may be their only meal for the day. The homeless consider Craig and Lacey to be their friends—people who care in their world that is so filled with the uncaring.

Terry loved to hang out at Craig's restaurant while he was in college. Not only were he and Craig good friends, but the restaurant was located next to the Louisiana Attorney General's Office. Harrington's Café was the special agents' favorite place to sit and chat about their cases over lunch. Terry made sure that he was there often enough that the agents got to know him.

Terry could talk to anyone, and he did. The guys soon began to encourage him, giving him advice on how to get into this elite agency. These agents were responsible for handling crimes and assisting local police with their unsolved cases. They worked on white-collar crimes, Internet crimes, cold murder cases and as bodyguards for dignitaries, among many other things. Terry was fascinated. He loved hearing the guys talk about their work. He wanted to be one of them. It became his burning desire.

But I think his passion for law enforcement started long before that. I remember one night when Terry was in ninth grade, he was hungry and decided to stop at McDonalds on his way home. Out of the corner of his eye, he noticed a gang of boys gathered in the parking lot. He didn't pay much attention to them, just walked by and went into the restaurant. After he had grabbed a bite to eat, the boys flagged Terry over. He was reluctant to go because he didn't like the looks of them, but he was afraid that if he ignored them, they might get offended. He cautiously walked over.

It was evident that one particular boy was the ringleader. He was a cocky little guy who had a gruff look. He thought Terry was someone else, another boy who had gone on a date with the girlfriend of one of the gang members, and he challenged Terry to a fight.

Terry informed them that they had the wrong guy, but by this time, the ring of boys had surrounded him. They beat him mercilessly, each taking turns punching and kicking. Then they left him there—hurt, bleeding, and barely able to move. He noticed that some people had witnessed the incident, but no one had come to his aid. He couldn't understand that. Even the sheriff's officer who was doing extra duty patrol at McDonald's that night did nothing. That officer later told us that he was on duty for McDonald's, and Terry was in the adjoining parking lot. Like that made a difference. I wanted to strangle him.

Terry made it back to his truck and drove home. We were horrified when we saw him. We brought him to the emergency room where they took X-rays and cleaned him up. He had a broken rib and was covered in bruises.

The next day, Terry Sr. paid a visit to the McDonald's, but the manager would take no responsibility for the assault. It took him a few days, but Terry learned the name of the little punk who had instigated the beating. Apparently, the boy had been on a rampage, and Terry had not been the only victim that night. Along with the two other sets of parents whose children had suffered at the hands of that gang that night, we pressed charges.

As I sat in the courtroom during the trial, I figured out what the problem was. I watched the boy's parents and how they related to him. They were as cold and heartless to their son as their son had been to Terry. You could see the hate in them. I was sure that he learned his mean behavior from them. They looked at us with hate in their eyes as if we had done something to them.

After the judge reviewed the evidence, he looked at us and the other families and gave us his sympathy. He then looked at the boy and told him that he would be going away for some time to learn how to behave in society. The boy was placed in a juvenile hall and assigned to do community service.

I was very proud of Terry that day for following through and not letting that gang get the best of him. His sense of justice, of right and wrong, had surfaced, and I think that is the moment that the seeds were planted for him to become a police officer.

Terry knew that he would have to acquire at least two years of police work before the attorney general's office would hire him—the guys had already clued him in on that prerequisite. He decided that he wanted to go to the Baton Rouge Police Department for his training. Following in the footsteps of his grandfather was important to him. Terry's goals were big. He wouldn't listen to any negatives or let anyone tell him that he couldn't make the grade. The agents in the attorney general's office knew that Terry wanted to work with them. They saw the tenacity and the drive that he had, and they knew that's what it took to be one of them. Terry fit in.

He applied to the city police department after graduating from college and was accepted.

Training was grueling. Sergeant Jeff LeDuff was his training officer. LeDuff was a black belt in karate, and you could tell that he was tough by the way he was built. He was strong, muscular and ran a tight ship. At six foot four inches, he had a stature that put fear on the cadet's faces. When he spoke, they listened. Training lasted for months. Terry jogged until he nearly passed out. He did pushups until his arms quivered. He worked hard, but when he finished, he was prepared for the streets of the city. But he had been preparing for this all of his life.

Just before Terry entered junior high, we had moved to a larger home that was situated on a few acres. The houses on either side of us were also large acreage lots so we didn't have the traditional neighborhood for the kids to play in. Cars usually sped down the highway that ran along the front of the property, and it wasn't safe for the kids to ride their bikes like they had done in the old neighborhood. I had to think of alternative activities for them to do so they wouldn't take off on their bikes down that busy road.

Luckily, there was a gym about a half-mile from our house, and Terry showed interest in joining. He loved it. He got more and more involved in exercise and learning about nutrition. The trainers there liked him, and although he was not paying them to train him, they always helped him by showing him the correct ways to work out.

I saw a change in Terry as a result. He became more aware of what he ate and began leaning toward lots of protein and well balanced meals. He would quote instructions about the various supplements that were good to take and how the body would benefit from them. At a young age, he learned the importance of keeping the body healthy and fit, and he continued to love exercise throughout his life. So although he was being subjected to intense physical workouts as part of his police academy training, that was something Terry actually enjoyed.

Just before graduation, LeDuff announced that he was going to treat all of the cadets to lunch. Terry asked him what color shirt he intended to wear for the occasion.

"Boy, I'm not going to tell you something stupid like that," LeDuff retorted.

"Come on," Terry persuaded with a grin. "I'm going to wear the same color as you."

"That's not going to happen, because I'm not going to tell you. Now, go on, boy," LeDuff ordered.

On the day of the luncheon, Terry drove to the restaurant and waited in his car for LeDuff to arrive. Armed with an assortment of shirts of every color in the back seat of his truck, he quickly pulled out a black shirt that was just like the one that LeDuff was wearing.

The look on the sergeant's face when he saw Terry wearing a matching shirt was hilarious. Although LeDuff knew that Terry was a prankster and enjoyed the joke, he didn't let Terry know. His stern look at being the butt of the joke gave the cadets something to laugh about, but it was Terry who laughed the loudest.

It wasn't long before LeDuff, who would later become chief, and Terry developed a special bond. Although their working relationship was bound by the confines of the hierarchy, they became friends. LeDuff could see that there was a special man inside this young police officer. As their mutual respect grew, Terry became more and more aware that he had been trained by the best.

As Terry moved out onto the streets, he was assigned to the roughest crime areas in the city. All of the rookies had to work their way up to the better districts. Terry buffered me from stories about the cases he worked. He knew that telling me what he was exposed to on a daily basis would only make me worry more than I already did.

During this time, I could tell that he was carrying a huge burden. I could see it in his face and hear it in his voice. The crime that he saw on the streets affected him. It was evil. He was surrounded by it every day—rapes and murders and the worst of what human beings can inflict upon each other. What disturbed him most was when criminals were arrested while their children cried in the background. I remember he once broke down the door of a suspected drug dealer. Drugs were spread all over, and the children were sitting among them in the filthy, bug-infested apartment. That really bothered him, that children are sometimes raised in such an environment.

This was a part of life to which he had never been exposed. After that particular incident, Terry made a decision that he would make a difference. He was going to speak his mind whenever the situation presented itself. He would tell everyone what worked for him—God. But sometimes making a difference could get him into trouble.

The rule of the department was that procedure was to be followed at all times. The well-being of these men was the police department's utmost priority. This rule escaped Terry one night when he was pumping gas and watched a drug deal happening right in front of him. After he finished pumping his gas, he approached the vehicle and dealer involved and at gunpoint arrested the drug dealer. Then he called for help.

When police units arrived, the officers found Terry holding the handcuffed drug dealer with the drugs on the front seat. Terry's supervisor was horrified that Terry had not followed procedure and called for help before apprehending this criminal. He was so upset that he led Terry to believe that he was going to demote him because of the risk that he had taken.

"But L.T., I just had to do it," Terry tried to explain. "It was right in front of me."

After carefully thinking it over, Lieutenant Larry Hayes, L.T. as Terry called him, decided to allow Terry to keep his position.

Terry's emotions had taken over his good sense and he had reacted, placing his life in danger. He was that passionate about what he did. But he knew better and realized that it had almost cost him his job.

He got a real lesson that day on the importance of procedure.

7

Sergeant Frankie Caruso grinned to himself as he listened to the detectives in his unit laughing about the latest gag that had been played. Someone had placed a plastic tie wrap around the drive shaft of one of the patrol cars so that when the motor started, the plastic made a loud thumping noise. It had taken the victim of this particular prank a while to figure out what was making the horrendous noise in the motor. Frankie had a suspicion about who had pulled the prank, although Terry had the same poker face he always had. It was difficult for Frankie to tell if it had been Terry, and he watched him for any telltale sign—a grin, a smirk—but Terry just laughed along with the other detectives and pretended to be innocent.

Frankie had always enjoyed Terry's sense of humor. He had known him since he was a baby, had held him in his arms soon after Terry was born. Terry Sr. had been one of Frankie's best friends throughout childhood. Together, they had grown into men, had ridden Harleys together, had gotten married, had children and then moved away from each other to different sections of town. But those years of friendship ran deep for both men, and they would recapture old times at the birthday parties of their children.

Frankie had been in the narcotics division of the Baton Rouge Police Department for twenty years when he ran into the younger Terry at an intelligence meeting. Terry told Frankie that he was interested in becoming a police officer and that he wanted to work in narcotics. Frankie was thrilled. The next time they met, Terry informed him that he had been accepted into the police academy. Frankie took it upon himself to keep an eye out for him.

"Don't forget about me now," Terry would say each time he'd see Frankie watching him train.

According to policy, an officer has to serve three years in uniform patrol before he can work in a specialized division. Terry spent those years learning the ropes, honing his skills and working hard to establish himself as a good and respected officer. He wanted to make an impression so that when his three years were complete, he would be accepted into narcotics right away.

"I saw him come up one day to put his letter in," Frankie recalled. "He told me he almost had his three years in, and he was ready. I told him that he had to go through procedure, but he was so excited. I remember he had just gotten a new rifle—an AR-15—that he wanted to show me. While I was looking at it, he asked me all about what narcotics was like. He was so interested in what we did in the unit. He interviewed and was chosen for my squad. I wanted him there. I knew firsthand what a good guy he was. I wanted to look after him."

While Terry was still in training, I ran into Frankie while having lunch at Semolina's one day. I was worried about Terry going into narcotics because I knew that it would be a much more dangerous job for him. I expressed my concern, and Frankie told me not to worry. "It's a good place to work," he reassured me. "I'll take him under my wing and look after him."

And Frankie did. Sometimes the other officers would rib him about it, but Frankie stood firm to his promise, teaching Terry what he needed to know about the job and watching out for him in dangerous situations.

At the time, there were twelve officers and three supervisors working the narcotics division. There was always an air of excitement in the office. Every detective knew the danger of the job and embraced it, thrived on it. They spent most days working with confidential informants (CIs), making drug buys, writing reports, tagging evidence.

The CIs would find out what kinds of drugs were being sold from a particular house and report it to the unit. The rule of thumb was usually that if someone had only a couple of ounces of marijuana, they would arrest the dealer, then try to get him to tell them who he had gotten it from. By flipping, as it is called, the smaller dealers, the detectives were able to work their way up the chain to the larger and more dangerous drug dealers.

Some days, the detectives would work their own cases, some days they would assist other detectives with theirs, and sometimes they would spend half of the day testifying in court against the dealers they had arrested. Business was booming in Baton Rouge, and there was never a shortage of cases to work.

At times, the detectives would have a CI meet with someone in a parking lot. The CI would be wired, and as soon as the deal went down, the detectives would swarm in and make the arrest. Other times, the CI would go to a dealer's house and make a buy while trying to determine when the next shipment would be coming in so that the narcotics unit could be informed. Many of the CIs were prostitutes, and the unit always tried to keep its CIs safe. They were not normally required to testify in court, and the detectives tried not to put them in environments that would be too unsafe.

When it was time to "hit a house," Frankie or one of the other supervisors would have a briefing to discuss how to proceed. With a search warrant in hand, the detectives would approach the house. Sometimes they would just knock on the door and wait for someone to answer before executing the warrant, but other times they would bring Buster, the battering ram, along and just bust through the door. It depended on the amount of drugs detectives suspected were inside or the amount of danger involved.

Each man in the unit was very aware of the danger involved with the job, and they all looked out for each other. Battering your way into the home of a criminal is always a risk. But everyone shared a common goal—to get drugs off the street. Each time an arrest was made and drugs were seized, that much less was available to a kid who might be tempted to delve into the unknown. Terry usually went a step further. When he would arrest a petty criminal, he would try to help that person. In the car on the way back to the unit, he would talk to the dealer and try to gauge why the person wanted to live that sort of life. Terry would talk about options, about another way of life, about how to get help, about God. Occasionally, he was successful. More often, he wasn't. But he never stopped trying.

"People responded to him," said Frankie. "He always had that big grin. He was a pretty boy, neat and always dressed nice. Even when he was at his worst, he still looked decent, and even criminals responded to him."

Always determined to do his best, Terry often asked Frankie to critique his performance on this bust or that. He wanted to do everything right. And he usually did, even when he was playing jokes.

"After we figured out he was the one orchestrating the pranks, we decided to get him. We were out on a warrant one day, and we brought a big ol' bag of baking powder along. After we searched the house and discovered nothing, we put the baking powder in a drawer. He found it and was so excited. He thought he had just found a big bag of cocaine. Back at the unit, we ragged him so much. We took pictures of him with the bag and hung them up with signs that read 'Fake Dope and Big Dope.' Terry took it all in stride and posed for those photos. He could take it as well as he could dish it out."

Frankie and Terry became good friends through working together. Frankie viewed him both as a son and a friend. He sometimes thought that it was interesting that he and Terry Sr. had always been such good friends and how much the young Terry had come to mean to him. Frankie was determined that he would keep his promise to me. Nothing would happen to my son. But our family was about to be turned inside out, nonetheless.

8

Things were going so well for everyone. Terry was living his dream. Lacey was happily married and building her own family. Kaylan was doing well in school and enjoying her young life. Terry Sr. and I were getting older together just as we had planned. But a routine annual visit with my doctor would change everything.

Getting a mammogram is uncomfortable, but a necessary evil for all women. I don't think we ever really think about it. We just do it, never thinking anything could be wrong—until we get "the call," as I did at the office at four-thirty one afternoon.

"Mrs. Melancon. Your mammogram revealed a suspicious mass that needs to be investigated. You will need to set up an appointment for a biopsy as soon as possible."

I sat very still, the phone receiver still in my hand. It was my thirty-ninth birthday. I had been trying to leave the office early to have a birthday dinner with my family. I just sat there. I couldn't think. Cancer is such a scary word. I decided not to say anything to anyone. I would deal with this tomorrow. I wanted to enjoy my birthday.

I laughed through dinner. *Do I have cancer?* I opened my presents. *Will I lose a breast?* I hugged my children. *Isn't chemotherapy painful? Will I lose my hair? Will my husband still love me?*

The next morning I called the doctor. He said he wanted me to see a surgeon as soon as possible. He instructed me to pick up my X-rays from his office and take them to the surgeon I had chosen. *What do you mean—the surgeon I have chosen? How do you choose a surgeon?*

When I told Terry Sr., he reacted as he always did. He is a practical man and reassured me that everything would be fine. "There's no need to overreact," he said. "I'm sure it will be just fine." He hugged me to him, and I felt better.

I picked up the phone book and began searching for a surgeon who could see me. When one told me it would be weeks before I could get an appointment, I went to the next. I finally reached a doctor who could see me the next day. After picking up the X-rays, I drove to her office. Before getting out of my car, I slowly opened the large envelope that housed the X-rays. I slid them out along with the notes from the radiologist who had read the film.

"Suspected malignant mass. Treatment recommended immediately," were the words I read.

This is going much too fast. In just two days, I go from a normal life to a suspected malignancy?

I walked with a feeling of dread into the doctor's office and was immediately brought back to the examination room. A young woman walked in with a physician's coat on, her name monogrammed on the right pocket. She was the doctor. She was young. Very young.

Before even examining me, she said the words I couldn't bear to hear. "It looks like you have cancer. I called your doctor before you came, and he agrees with me that it is probably cancer and needs to come out. You need surgery. How does tomorrow sound?"

Hold up! Can't I think about this? How can you be sure? What about my family?

As I told her to schedule it, I realized that I was crying hysterically. Between my sobs, she told me that she was going to do a needle localization procedure and then excise the mass to get enough tissue to ensure clear margins. In layman's terms, she was going to find the mass by inserting long—very long—needles into me and then X-ray the needles to help her locate the mass. She said she was going to remove the mass along with the surrounding tissue until she found no more signs of the cancerous tissue. She would have a pathologist there to help determine clear margins.

I had to tell my children. I didn't know how to tell them.

With fear in my heart, I got up the next morning knowing that my life was about to change. The needle localization was extremely painful. But after that procedure, the surgery went well. While I was still in recovery, my doctor told my family that everything had gone smoothly and that the way she saw it, it didn't look like cancer at all. That was such a relief. After spending a few hours in recovery, I was moved to a room and was able to go home the next day.

No cancer! What a close call. That was so scary. I went back to work, and my life resumed as normal until the third day after my surgery. The doctor called my husband before I got home to tell him what she was about to tell me. Terry Sr. was already coming up the driveway when I received the call. He had tears rolling down his face. It was the first time I had ever seen him cry.

"Mrs. Melancon, I've made a mistake. It was cancer. I am so sorry. We need to talk about further surgery."

I heard nothing else.

One by one, my kids came home, and I had to tell them. The looks on their faces was far more painful for me than any surgery could ever be.

Terry wept.

Lacey tried to be strong. I knew it was just for me.

Kaylan dropped her head to hide her tears.

It was obvious that they were looking to me for my reaction. With all the strength I could muster, I boldly told them that this was all going to be fine. I said that we would get through this. Kaylan asked me what was next. I told her surgery and then chemo.

"Does that mean you are going to lose your hair?"

"Probably," I said.

For a teenager, that thought was devastating. I could tell by her reaction.

"Just think of the money we'll save on shampoo, and besides now it will only take me five minutes in the morning to get ready," I quipped as bravely as I could.

"Yeah, Mom. It's not like you had great hair anyway," Terry said in his most serious voice. Everyone just looked at him. His expression was priceless, and that turned into a moment that was precious to me. He had taken the pain from my daughters' faces and replaced it with laughter.

I knew that it was time to get busy fighting this huge monster. I needed to find the best doctor for me, one who specialized in this kind of cancer. I called my cousin, Terri, whose husband, Doctor Kevin Settig, is a well known surgeon in Shreveport, Louisiana. He was willing to help any way he could. Kevin specialized in surgery for burn patients, but he had many friends who were physicians in the Baton Rouge area and promised he would get their advice.

Dr. Benton Dupont was the chief of surgery at Baton Rouge General Hospital, specializing in oncology surgery. He was recommended by several of Kevin's friends. He agreed to see me the next day and performed the surgery to remove the mass several days later. He was clearly the best doctor for me. He was aggressive with his treatment and worked closely with an oncologist that had been highly recommended to me as well—Dr. David Hansen.

My cancer had spread to my lymphatic system, which was not a good sign. Thirty-two lymph nodes were removed, with more than sixteen being cancerous. My doctor explained that it did not look good, even with chemo and radiation treatments. My future was in God's hands.

I went through almost a year of treatment. I felt like the medicine they were giving me to save my life was killing me. Chemo was mean stuff. The nurses called this particular medicine that had the color of bright red blood "the red devil." This was the final medicine in my treatment and was known for making patients very sick. The patients who had the red bag hanging from the IV pole had a sickly, pale look. It was the look of death. I told them that I preferred to call it the blood of Jesus running through my veins. I wanted no part of anything other than Jesus, who could choose to heal me or not. I knew I would accept either choice with dignity.

But there were many tests along the way—times when I had to be strong, not only for me, but for everyone else. I remember being at the wedding of a close friend with my husband and the kids. We were sitting together in the pew of the church when I gently pushed my hair out of my face and noticed that a handful of hair was in my hand. It was falling out. All I could do was gently pat it to my head and hope and pray that it wasn't noticeable.

Later, as people were dancing around me, all I could think of was that if I start shaking my head my hair was going to be gone, all of it in front of my friends. I was petrified and told my husband my dilemma. He wanted to know if I wanted to go home. I wasn't about to let this big "C" monster steal my fun. I declined and visited with my friends as if nothing were happening. When we finally got home, I told the kids.

Terry said that he had noticed some clumps of hair around the house, but thought that our dog, Chelsea, a five-pound Yorkie, had started shedding.

"Mom, I don't mean that you have dog hair or nothing, but, ya know, you and Chelsea have that dark hair with a little gray mixed in. I mean, whenever you don't color your hair…I mean, sometimes, Mom…" he stuttered.

He knew he was getting in deep, and I quickly rescued his attempt to make me feel better.

"I know what you mean. It's okay. I'll admit that my hair is chemically dependant. I love you. I'm fine with this."

I needed to be fine or at least tell to them that I would be. They viewed me as their emotional barometer. If this bothered me, then it would have been devastating to them. It took all that I had to hold it in and be strong. But that's what I did.

"Terry, go and get the scissors from the kitchen drawer," I ordered. "Kaylan, get a towel. Lacey help me carry a kitchen stool to the backyard. Now who wants to be first?"

Terry Sr. sat in a chair on the patio and watched. When I would look his way, he would turn his head, not wanting me to see that he had tears in his eyes.

No one wanted to be first, so I grabbed a clump of hair to cut it, but just the slightest tug made it come right out.

They watched in amazement. My hair really didn't need cutting. It just came out on its own. Terry stroked my head and retrieved a clump, as did Lacey and Kaylan. The scissors were used only to clip the remanding strands. Within a few moments, it was gone. My stool was surrounded with piles of dark brown hair. Sitting there with the kids gently stroking my head and wads of hair falling down around me made me feel so loved.

I resembled a mangy dog because several stubborn patches of hair had clung in place in the funniest spots. I touched my head and gasped at the smoothness of it.

My world brightened in that backyard that afternoon. They were there for me, to love me and see me through this. It always takes moments like this—the ones we think are the most devastating events in our lives—to truly make us appreciate what is most valuable to us.

9

The large chemotherapy room that housed thirty or more leather recliners was filled with cancer patients getting their injections for hours on end. This went on every three weeks for seven months. Every time I walked into that room, I saw the same faces, although occasionally there was a new face with eyes reflecting the terror of the unknown.

The faces of the people sitting in those chairs always tugged at my heart. They were from all walks of life—a cowboy sitting there with his wife, a young girl crying because her hair had started to fall out, an elderly man whose wife read to him from *Reader's Digest* while he dozed off. Meanwhile the nurses busily addressed beeping IVs and handed pans to the ones who couldn't keep anything down.

I felt drawn to talk to them, to listen to their stories and try to help. I called it "pole surfing." After getting my meds and getting a short nap to wear off some of the sleeping medicine, I would wake, unplug my pole and start walking. I knew that I had a certain amount of time on the battery of the intravenous pole before I had to recharge it. Everyone had a story, and I loved learning about the people behind the disease.

I can remember sitting there with an elderly lady who was reclining in her chair. She was bundled up in a cotton thermal blanket. At first,

I thought she wanted to be alone. She seemed to be going to sleep, but when I stopped in front of her, she heard the squeak of my IV pole and opened her eyes. She smiled at me and asked me to sit beside her.

"My name is Helen Wesley," she informed me.

"I'm pleased to meet you, Ms. Helen. Is it okay if I call you that?"

"Sure, honey, what's your name?"

"Vicki."

"Well, what you here for, honey?"

"Breast cancer," I said.

"I got this bone cancer that spread. They say it's all over. This is my third time going through this treatment stuff. I sure am tired," she said, pulling her blanket closer.

"Who brings you here for treatment, Ms. Helen?"

"My niece. The nurses call her when I'm about done and she waits downstairs for me."

You could tell that she had lived a hard life. Her clothes were worn and very outdated. Her hair was braided on top of her head, and her face was drawn and wrinkled. It looked to me like she was much older than her years. I had noticed that she was alone most of the time.

I soon learned that Ms. Helen had acquired a wealth of wisdom throughout her life. We talked about her family and mine. She had a faith that was genuine. She spoke about God like she knew Him personally. I wondered it I could ever get to the point where I could hear from Him and trust Him like Ms. Helen did. She spoke in a strong southern drawl, and at times, I could barely understand her. But I carefully read her lips so that I would not miss a word she said.

She often spoke of her life as a housemaid for a wealthy family. She said that the family didn't know anything about love, that they used money to satisfy that hole in their lives.

"Those poor children, they ain't got no love. They just get more and more stuff. That mama and dad just keep saying that they ain't got any time. Them are some good kids, but they ain't gonna be for long if someone don't take some time and love them. I don't understand people these days."

This would usually lead into a conversation about her daughter. "She calls sometimes, lives in Virginia. She's an accountant. I worked hard to put her through school. I felt real bad when she had to get a few loans to get through school but I paid for most of it. It's just sometimes I was a little low on money, and I couldn't. Maybe that's the reason she doesn't call that much. Or maybe she's embarrassed that I didn't get much education." Ms. Helen would sigh and go on, "But I do love her, and I miss her. One day she will know how much I love her. Anyway, some of these people in here are not very friendly."

I searched her out whenever I went for treatment, but within a few weeks, she no longer came. I asked the nurses what happened to her and was told that she had passed away. I hope Ms. Helen knew how much I loved her and how much I miss her. I do know that when I get to heaven, I will certainly see that kind, wise old woman there.

The pole surfing went on for the whole time I was in treatment. I seemed to always find someone who needed to talk. Talking is usually what I do best, but I learned that during moments such as these that listening is more important. The patients didn't want pity; they wanted to talk to someone who shared their feelings, their fears, their pains.

We compared our diseases and shared the symptoms we were having like we were comparing battle wounds. It was common ground. I tried to be positive and to lift them up as best I could. Most of the people had a wonderfully positive attitude. It was amazing to see this. These people had every reason to be down on life, to blame someone or to curl up with their pity party, but many were living their lives to the fullest.

I learned a lot during that time. There is a passage in the Bible that says, "When I am weak, then I am strong." I know what God was saying. The weakest time in my life gave me strength. I became strong in an emotional way. I learned to lean on God as I could no longer lean on anyone else. He brought me to a position of total dependency on Him. I became a stronger human being, a better human being.

Here we all were fighting to stay alive, but, really, isn't that's what life's all about? Every day that goes by is one day closer to the end of our lives. It's strange what goes through your mind when you are reminded of the fragility of your own life. I know that I never thought about how my life would end, about what my death would be like. I thought that when I got really old, I would just not wake up one morning, and then I would be gone. In my new world, I knew my death could be very different. I learned that cancer does not know a stranger, that anyone's life can be turned upside down in a mere second just by the mention of that word.

And then it was over. I ended my cancer treatment with a graduation ceremony. That was one of the best days of my life. I had made it through. I'm a survivor. I fought a fierce battle and won. I knew that nothing could ever bring me down again. I had so much to live for and suddenly had a new appreciation for my husband and my children who had pulled me through this ordeal.

Several months later, I was invited to a Christmas brunch hosted by my friend, Linda Gaspard. Linda is a very successful realtor in our city, and she hosts an annual Christmas brunch for her friends and clients. Her invitation suggested that everyone bring a white elephant gift. After asking several people what that was, I was informed that it was a gag gift that was to be exchanged with the others at the brunch that day.

About seventy or eighty women attended the event, and before long we were all laughing at the silly gifts we received and trying to exchange our gifts for better ones by stealing from one another. After the gift exchange stopped, we ate a wonderful spread of foods and desserts.

While I was walking out, the girl who stole my gift walked with me, and we laughed about what fun the party had been. She looked familiar and commented that she thought she knew me.

"Are you Mrs. Melancon?" she said.

"Yes. You're Doctor Crain, aren't you?"

"Yes I am."

"You're the doctor who did my surgery several years ago," I said as the realization set in.

"I remember you well, Mrs. Melancon."

Of course she did. This was the young doctor who had made the mistake of telling me that I had no cancer when I did. My cousin, Kevin, had told us later that she had been very distraught after that incident and that her office knew all about the mistake she had made.

"Mrs. Melancon, I have thought about you so much over these last few years. How are you doing?"

"I'm doing fine. I've thought about you, too."

I told her that I knew it must have been hard for her and that I wanted her to know that I had forgiven her.

"Thank you, Vicki," she said. "I needed to hear that."

We hugged each other for a moment, both of us wiping the tears from our eyes. It was a wonderful Christmas. That incident reminded me that I was cancer-free and that God had a plan for my future. He was teaching me how to tackle my monsters.

Not long after, as I was driving to a store on a Wednesday evening, I had to pass a church that I had passed dozens of times before. I usually tried to avoid going that route because when church was in session, the traffic was backed up for miles. I had always thought that was very strange, especially on a Wednesday night. I had never gone to church in the middle of the week. I barely made it on Sundays, but this church seemed to have so much traffic that it was necessary to have several policeman directing incoming cars. Healing Place Church was the name that always caught my attention. While I was sitting in that line of traffic, I thought that it might be a good idea to see what attracted all these people to this particular church. I called home and told the kids that I was going to be a little late, but I didn't tell them I was going to church. I thought I would just go in and sit in the back. I was hoping to find a little comfort, maybe something that would help stem all the fear I had been feeling.

Dressed in everyday clothes with a bandana covering my still-bald head, I walked in and was greeted at the front door by a young man who was very handsomely dressed. He smiled as I took a brochure from him. It was not like anything I had ever seen. I took a seat in the back of the auditorium-like building and watched. The people were gathered in friendly groups talking and laughing. They seemed to know almost everyone who passed and shook their hands or embraced them as they made their way to their seats. Most of the people there were young adults. I was amazed of the number of young couples and teenagers who were having a great time talking to their friends.

The church that I had attended all my life was very solemn. People didn't talk or laugh, and the atmosphere was not friendly. This was certainly different. As I sat there silently observing, several ladies approached me and welcomed me warmly. The kindness that I saw was so genuine. They invited me to sit with them and made me feel at home.

The minute I had walked in, I had felt peace. I left that church that night knowing that I had found what I was looking for, what I had always been looking for. I knew now why so many people worshipped there. It was obvious. I felt God there.

The pastor, Dino Rizzo, was a thirty-year-old man, with a beautiful wife, DeLynn, and two small children. It was apparent that Pastor Dino was very much in love with his wife but on occasion he used her in his sermon to get a point across. You could see that she loved him, too, because she only laughed each time he used her as an example.

The sermon that night was about the Bible, something that I knew little about, but I found myself wanting to know more. I went back the next week, and the next, but always alone. I had not yet shared this discovery with my family. I wanted to hold it to myself for a while, just to make sure it was real.

Because I had raised my children in the more traditional church, they thought mom had gone off into the deep end of a lake when I finally shared my secret with them. I tried to tell them that they should try it, but the more I talked about the church, the more they resisted. They respected that I went there but made it clear that I shouldn't expect them to go.

Soon they saw a change in me. I became a more patient, peaceful and loving person. I was different. I quit trying to convince them to go to this wonderful place I had discovered and just let them make their own decisions.

It wasn't long before all of my children were there with me. Terry, Lacey and Kaylan would sit beside me every Sunday on that pew, each one experiencing what I had that first time. I watched them each change in a wonderful way. Their faith became stronger. They were more at peace. Like me, they had truly discovered God. After the struggle we had each gone through dealing with my cancer, finally our lives had once again become good.

I didn't know how badly we would one day need that faith or how important that church would become in our lives. But in just a few short years we would find out.

10

"I knew that I was going to meet you that day."
"What are you talking about?" Lynn asked.
"I'll tell you some day. Not today," Terry replied.
"I love you, baby."
"Me too."

TERRY BEGAN WEARING GLASSES when he was seven years old, and his eyesight progressively worsened through the years. In high school, he wore hard contact lenses because the soft ones simply would not correct his vision. His doctor said that when he was old enough, he could have corrective surgery. He was about sixteen when the doctor decided that it would be a good time to try the surgery.

For the most part, it was a success. Terry's vision improved, but he experienced what some patients call "starbursts" at night. He described streetlights or headlights on cars as if he were seeing a dramatic burst of light coming at him. At the time, we could do nothing about this, and Terry learned to compensate and live with it.

After being accepted into the police force, he worked many night shifts. The starburst effect that he had learned to live with became a problem with his work. It blurred his vision at night, and it became crucial that he do something about it. He needed to be able to see at night. Working in crime-infested neighborhoods and running raids on drug dealers was hard enough. Any deficit in his vision could be fatal to him or another policeman.

His eye doctor suggested that Terry see Dr. Daniel at the eye clinic at Memorial Hospital in New Orleans for the surgery. Dr. Daniel had perfected an operation to correct this problem. Many patients simply lived with this deficiency, and most decided against surgery because the technology was new and the surgery was experimental. Terry could not take that chance. His poor night vision could cost lives.

Dr. Daniel was a petite lady with a soft voice who was confident she could rectify Terry's problem. Her confidence impressed him, and he scheduled the surgery, unaware that it would change his life.

On the day of the surgery, Terry's friend, Jimmy Sandridge, drove him, as Terry would be receiving local anesthesia during the procedure and would be unable to drive himself home. Terry knew it was going to be a good day. As they drove past small towns like St. Gabriel and Donaldsonville and Gonzales, Terry informed Jimmy that things were about to change.

"I'm going to meet someone today, someone who will be perfect for me," he announced. "God told me that I would. Just wait and see."

"Yeah right, Terry. Sure you are."

"Okay, buddy, just wait and see. I'm going to meet a girl who is going to be a knockout."

"You're dreaming, you big fool," Jimmy laughed.

"I'm telling you, Jimmy. I'm going to meet someone at this clinic today. I know it."

"Whatever. I'm hungry. Let's stop to eat."

Jimmy was always hungry. He was more than six-feet-four-inches tall and just a big guy. He and Terry were eating buddies and had been best friends in high school. They had belonged to the same gym ever since. Every day after school or work, the boys would go to the gym and work out.

Weight lifting and strength building became a competition between them. If one lifted two hundred fifty pounds, the other would have to lift two hundred sixty pounds or he would be subjected to the dreaded weakling jokes they enjoyed hurling at each other.

When they were younger, sometimes the jokes would result in a brawl in the backyard with the two of them rolling and wrestling on the ground until I came out and broke it up or one of them gave up and stomped off.

After their workout, the two of them would usually grab a bite to eat. Eating was a hobby they both enjoyed enormously. They chose restaurants specifically for their buffets. They didn't want to be limited to just one plate; they wanted as many as they could fill with as much food and as many desserts as possible. Restaurants lost money when Terry and Jimmy walked through their doors. All-you-can-eat specials were perfect for their insatiable appetites. They would walk out of a restaurant wobbling and rubbing their bellies, all the while laughing about how much they had consumed.

The friendship between Terry and Jimmy was strong, and after Jimmy married and moved to another part of town, he and Terry continued to hang out and go to the gym almost every day.

They also shared similar occupations. Jimmy was a deputy sheriff for East Baton Rouge Parish. He was responsible for booking prisoners into the parish prison. And he had always been willing to do anything for Terry, which is why on this day he had taken off of work to drive Terry to New Orleans.

"How do you know that you are going to meet someone today?" he teased Terry as they continued their drive. "God told you?"

"Yep."

"You're crazy, man," Jimmy said, shaking his head.

It took them a little over an hour to reach the hospital. Terry was checked in and led to the procedure room after filling out the necessary pre-surgery paperwork. Several nurses prepared his eyes with special liquid drops. Dr. Daniel came in and completed the surgery within just a few minutes.

When she was finished, she sat Terry up to check his vision. It was close to perfect. The operation was a success. She laid him back down on the table and put ice packs on both of his eyes. She instructed him that he needed to lie there for a while. She said she would have a nurse come in to check his blood pressure and to administer more drops in his eyes. She dimmed the lights slightly and left Terry on the table.

Lynn Harwell was a nurse at the hospital. Memorial Hospital was only a few minutes from where she lived in Chalmette, which is in the southeast part St. Bernard Parish and runs along the Mississippi River. The hospital's eye clinic specialized in Lasik surgery, as well as the new corrective procedure for patients with Terry's problem.

Dr. Daniel saw Lynn in the hall as she walked away from Terry's room. She told her that she had just performed surgery on a man that Lynn needed to meet. "He's very sweet, adorable really," the doctor said.

The comment struck Lynn as a bit odd. Dr. Daniel had never done this before. In fact, they rarely had occasion to speak to each other. Lynn was usually in the adjoining operating room and was assigned to another physician.

"I don't think so. I don't date patients," Lynn responded.

"You have to see this guy," Dr. Daniel persisted. "He is so nice and cute. Just go in and say hello."

"Thanks, but no thanks," Lynn laughed. "I have work to do."

Lynn was a natural beauty. Her long blonde hair and her deep brown eyes were warming. Even wearing surgical scrubs with a mask hanging around her neck, she was beautiful.

After she had finished with her patient and prepared for the next, Lynn headed for the break room. As she entered, she saw several of her friends with Dr. Daniel talking and laughing and having fun. The minute they saw Lynn, they ganged up on her. They told her she would regret it if she didn't go see this guy.

"It's time for his eye drops," Dr. Daniel chimed in. "Go. Just put the drops in for me."

"You girls are relentless," Lynn laughed. "You know the rules about dating patients."

"But technically, he's not your patient, right?" said the doctor.

"Okay," Lynn relented. "Give me the drops."

"You'll thank us for this."

Terry was still lying on the table when Lynn walked in. She watched as he moved at the sound of someone entering the room. He smiled as she approached, and she was immediately taken aback by his looks. She had not expected such a warm smile. She took in his dark hair, his muscular body. She took a deep breath.

"Mr. Melancon, I need to take your blood pressure and then put eye drops in your eyes. Can I help you up just a little bit to get your pressure?"

Terry slowly took off his eye packs and looked at Lynn. He smiled again. His dark, almost black eyes melted her. Lynn nervously took his blood pressure and asked how he was feeling.

"Great, now," Terry teased.

Lynn finished taking his blood pressure and told him that she would be sending in his nurse to go over the procedure for his care for the next few days.

Terry's nurse, Raquel, was a cute Latin woman with a heavy accent. Raquel finished her routine follow-up instructions and told Terry she would get his discharge papers so he could go home.

"Raquel, do you think you could get that blonde nurse that just took my blood pressure to check me out?"

"You mean Lynn? Sure, I'll be right back."

Raquel could hardly contain herself when she saw Lynn in the hall still waiting for her next patient.

"You are never going to believe this, Lynn, but he wants you to check him out."

"I'll bet he does."

" No, he wants you to discharge him. He asked for you."

"Raquel, you'd better not be kidding me."

"I'm dead serious. Now go."

Terry was sitting on the side of the hospital bed grinning like a Cheshire cat when Lynn walked back into his room, but he was nervous. He looked at her and prayed that he would not fumble his words when he spoke. He looked down at the ground and looked up at Lynn before he could choke out the words.

"May I ask you a personal question?" he finally said.

"Sure, go ahead."

"Can I take you out to dinner sometime?"

"I'd like that," Lynn said, writing her phone number on a piece of paper and handing it to him.

On the ride home, Terry told Jimmy about her.

"I met someone, and I'm going to marry her," Terry informed him.

"Just go to sleep," Jimmy responded. "I think that anesthesia has gotten to you."

Terry leaned back in his seat with a smile on his face.

During the next week, Terry planned how he was going to approach Lynn. He thought calling too soon would make him look desperate, but waiting too long would make her feel like he wasn't interested. He decided to call her in the middle of the week.

When her phone rang, Lynn saw the 225 prefix on the caller ID and wondered who would be calling her from Baton Rouge. Then she remembered the cute patient, and her pulse quickened.

"Lynn, this is Terry, the patient..."

"I know who you are," she jumped in. "How are you doing? How are your eyes?"

"Great. My eyes are much better. I was wondering if you had time for dinner this weekend?"

"I'm on call at the hospital this weekend," she said.

"Okay. We can do it another time." Terry's voice reflected his disappointment.

"What about the next weekend?" Lynn said.

Terry rebounded. "Well, my niece, Amelia, is turning one on Saturday. Would you want to come with me to her birthday party, and then we can grab a bite to eat after? But I have to warn you, the whole family will be there, including grandmas and grandpas, but they're really harmless. Birthdays in our family are big affairs. The who's who of the one-year-olds in the area will be invited—an elite group of toddlers, according to Amelia, and of course, the family members, including over ten or more cousins all under the age of eleven. Are you sure you would want to tackle this for our first date?"

"I'm willing, if you think they won't mind if I come."

"Are you kidding? You'll be one of the family before we leave. Trust me, my mom invites everyone to our parties, even people whose last name she doesn't know. She includes anyone and loves to surprise Dad with an occasional new face or two. One Christmas, Mom met someone at work who had just moved here from up north. She invited her to Christmas dinner and didn't mention it to my dad until she arrived. With my dad, it's always easier to ask forgiveness than permission. She'll ask you to go shopping with her and for a girls' night out before you leave. Trust me."

Lynn couldn't resist his appeal. "Okay. I'll drive in to Baton Rouge next Saturday around noon." She hesitated for a second then said, "I can't wait to see you, Terry."

"Me too."

They talked on the phone every night until the day of the party. I don't know what it was that drew them together so quickly. It was as if they were supposed to be together. They both felt an instant closeness that seemed surreal. This was something special. This was different.

Terry, the Burger Man

Lacey, Craig, Kaylan and Terry

Terry at ten years old on the Pirates baseball team

Terry playing ball in our backyard

Terry on a fishing trip with bait dangling from his mouth

Terry enjoying a vacation on a Cruise ship

Terry posing with Chief Jeff LeDuff the day he graduated from the police academy.

Me and Terry

Terry on the deck at the family camp

Lynn and Terry

Lacey and Terry

Craig, Terry Sr., Lacey, Kaylan, Vicki and Terry

Amelia and her uncle Terry

Grandpaw Melancon, Terry and Terry Sr.

The poem Terry wrote on envelopes just before he died

11

Saturday couldn't arrive fast enough for Terry. He smiled a big, happy smile when he saw Lynn pull up and went to greet her.

"Ready for a mega dose of the fam?" he laughed

I'm ready if you are," Lynn responded.

Gracie, Lacey's oldest daughter, ran to greet her uncle. At two, she loved to play dress up and had decided to dress herself for her sister's party. She had chosen a beautiful Cinderella ball gown, flowing with purple toile and sequins, a costume she had received for a Christmas present. Her green frog rubber boots finished the outfit with flair. Amelia wore her favorite princess tiara and a skirt made of the same fluffy toile that Gracie wore. The two of them were quite a pair.

Lacey was a terrific mother who knew to choose her battles with her children carefully. She quickly realized that letting the girls express themselves through their flamboyant costumes was harmless. They certainly earned a lot of attention for them, especially when they insisted on dressing up for church or to go to the grocery store. Most of the attention was from adults who had to comment on how beautiful their dresses were. Lacey knew that their admirers were just being kind, but

Gracie and Amelia basked in the attention and wanted to dress up all the time. This day was to be no different.

By the time Terry and Lynn arrived, the house was already getting full. Terry meandered his way through the crowd, introducing Lynn along the way until he found a seat for them on the stairs. They sat and watched.

I came in from the kitchen and walked over. Terry introduced Lynn to me. My first impression was that she was shy. She spoke softly and smiled genuinely. I liked her immediately. I could see that Terry saw something special in her. With time, I would learn that she was a very warm and caring person. For the moment, I was happy to see my son with someone who made him happy. If he liked her, I knew that I would accept her as well. I knew that time would reveal if she was the girl for him.

And it certainly did. They were together every weekend after that. The more he saw her, the more he fell in love with her. Lynn felt the same way.

"Lynn, I've waited for thirty years for you. I'm not going to let you go," Terry would say to her.

"You don't have to worry about that," she reassured him.

Their weekends were normally spent with us at our family camp on the Diversion Canal. One by one, our kids would arrive on Saturdays to spend the day with us. Between the jet skis and boats, there was always something fun to do, and food was always plentiful. Barbecued anything was their favorite, but they also enjoyed crawfish or crab boils when the shellfish were in season. After a big meal, we would all take a long boat ride on our party barge, slowly going upriver to watch the beautiful sunset. These moments were perfection.

Terry loved to Jet Ski. He enjoyed giving rides to everyone, especially if they didn't know how crazy he was. He would drive the Jet Ski in circles, making it almost impossible for anyone on the back to hold on. I had been a victim only once. It took a long while, but eventually he asked if I wanted to get on again. He looked so timid when he asked that I had to relent.

"Only if you behave yourself and drive safely. Do you promise?"

"Just get on, Mom. I'm not going to do anything."

I should have known from previous experience that the sweet little shyness routine he used was his way of getting unsuspecting victims on to give them the ride of their lives.

"Okay, but no crazy stuff."

I climbed on and held tightly to his life jacket.

"Hold on tight, Mom." I could hear his laughter as he took off, cutting a circle and splashing everyone on the deck.

I'd been had! Again!

He did everything in his power to make me scream. He cut circles back and forth, making me clutch tightly to his life jacket with all the energy I had. The more I yelled, the louder he laughed. Everyone on the deck was rolling right along with him.

Lacey and Kaylan were telling each other, "Mom's going to kill him."

I have to admit that it was so much fun, just being on the back with him, hanging on for dear life and watching him enjoying playing with me. He was so much fun to be around. He made me laugh.

After Lynn saw the torture that Terry put his riders through she was a little leery, but she agreed to ride with him. Surprisingly, he behaved himself. He didn't want to do anything wrong with her.

Lynn soon became a member of our family. When Terry came to visit alone, we wondered where she was. They became almost inseparable.

Lynn was a bit hesitant to bring Terry to meet her dad, Ellis, since she was the baby of the family and the only girl. Her dad didn't like most of the guys she'd brought home. Her mom, Gaynell, was much more accepting. Lynn felt like she had to set the stage for Terry before she brought him home. She wanted her family to like him.

"Now, dad, I really like this guy. Please try to be easy on him. I think you are going to like him. Will you at least try?" she begged.

"We'll see." Ellis was a man of few words.

That weekend when Terry arrived at Lynn's house, her mom made Terry feel right at home. Gaynell told Lynn that her dad was trying to fix a leak in the hall bathroom that had started that morning. She informed Lynn that he was a bit agitated. Terry could hear the clinging of tools and groans from the open door in the hall.

Lynn told Terry that it would probably be best if he waited until her dad was finished, but Terry got up and walked to the doorway of the bathroom

"Hello, Mr. Harwell. I'm Terry Melancon."

He was met with silence.

"What kind of problem do you have there?"

"A leak," was all Terry got and then silence again.

Terry could usually talk to anyone, but Ellis wasn't buying this boyfriend trying to date his little girl. He had already made up his mind about Terry up long before he had arrived.

"I can do a little plumbing," Terry tried again. "You mind if I take a look?

"Sure. What the heck?"

Ellis slid from under the cabinet and washed off his hands before shaking Terry's. Terry smiled that big cheesy grin that he always had on his face, and Ellis nodded.

"You don't have to do that, son. I'll get to it a little later."

"I don't mind. Let me see what ya got here." Terry studied the leak for a moment. "I see what the problem is. Can you hand me that wrench? You wouldn't happen to have any electrical tape or something that is waterproof?"

"I think I do in the garage. I'll go check."

Terry and Ellis spent the afternoon fixing the broken plumbing, and in the process became fast friends. Ellis loved Terry. Lynn always said that Terry was the only man she had ever brought home that her dad truly liked.

Gaynell loved him, too. She watched her daughter become a very happy girl, and she knew the reason why Lynn was so happy.

One weekend, Terry and Lynn rented Harley Davidson motorcycles for the day. Frankie Caruso and Phil Daigle joined them. They rode by the camp and showed us "this magnificent piece of metal," as Terry described it.

"I'm going to get one of these very soon," he said.

They decided to drive toward New Orleans. Along the way, Frankie and Phil went one way and Terry and Lynn went another.

Terry stopped the bike to take a rest. As they sat down, Terry got a very serious look on his face.

"I want to spend the rest of my life with you. How do you feel about that?" he said.

"I feel the same way, Terry. I love you, and I would go anywhere you go."

"I knew that I was going to meet you that day."

"What are you talking about?" Lynn asked.

"I'll tell you some day. Not today," Terry replied.

"I love you, baby."

"Me too."

Terry was not prepared for the official down on one knee will-you-marry-me moment, but that would come later when they picked out the perfect ring. For now, they both knew that they would be together forever.

Terry put his thumbs and index fingers to form a diamond shape and asked, "What do you think of those diamonds that look like that?'

"You mean a marquis?"

"I guess. Do you like those? I think they are pretty cool."

"I just want something simple. Whatever you decide will be perfect."

Terry passed away just weeks after this conversation. The ring was in its box in his house when he died. Lynn still wears it today and will treasure it for the rest of her life.

12

How do dozens of crickets get into a police car in the middle of the night?

That was the question the squad had the night that one of the detectives in the squad found himself serenaded by the pesky creatures while out on patrol. The noise was driving him crazy. It was dark, and they were hidden from sight. As soon as he would catch one, the others would begin to chirp even louder.

"If I catch the idiot who did this…just wait," he fumed as he lunged for another bug.

For the first time in a very long time the guy who liked to play pranks on everyone had been had. He had built for himself a reputation for playing practical jokes, and the guys never knew what he was going to come up with next. If shredded newspaper filled the inside of one of the police cars, everyone immediately knew who the culprit was. Shredded newspaper was one of his favorite jokes to play. He had perfected this little trick so well that he knew exactly how to do it without having any spillage to warn the victim what was waiting inside the car.

He would always let the other officers know when to go to the window to watch his victim of the day discover his surprise, and everyone would watch as the current victim approached the car with one hand in his pocket searching for his keys. While he was putting the key into the lock, his eyes noticed the car was full of paper. His hand dropped. He shook his head and looked around, trying to identify the culprit.

Those watching jumped out of view as he looked their way. No one wanted to be blamed for such a mess.

Not wanting to give the prankster any more satisfaction than he had already received, this particular victim opened the car door as heaps of paper fell out onto the ground. He scooped an armful out and jumped into the car. Paper was still attached to the door as he sped off, swirling in the car's dust.

The guys inside were rolling as they saw his head poking out of all of that paper as he tried to drive.

Terry was one of those laughing, but he, too, had been a victim of the prankster. He had reported to work one day only to find his locker filled with the same shredded paper. And not long before that, his chair had been rigged to break when he sat it in. Terry may have been the new kid on the block, but the practical joker had underestimated his talent and love for retaliation.

Stakeouts could be very boring. Before any arrests are made, it is customary in narcotics to watch a house or neighborhood for any suspicious activity for hours or days or longer.

On one particular night, several of the detectives were assigned to sit in a neighborhood at strategic locations. The detectives met at the station before dark and went over the game plan. Everything was choreographed, and everyone had an assignment. They chatted and sat around the office until it was time to go.

Terry went to grab some snacks and told the gang that he would be back in a few minutes. When he returned, everyone hurried to their units and proceeded to the assigned subdivision where they settled in for what they each knew would be a long night.

As soon as the sun went down, the detective noticed that the crickets were really making a ruckus.

I've heard crickets at night, but tonight they seem like they are right beside me. They sure can make noise.

He checked his windows to make sure none were rolled down.

How can it be so noisy when the windows are up?

He jumped.

What just landed on my knee? What was that? A cricket. How did that get in here?

He rolled down the window to throw it out when he noticed several crickets on his dashboard, and the noise from under the seat was getting louder. He grabbed a pen he carried in his unit that had a tiny flashlight on the end and looked around the seats and floorboard of the car.

Crickets. Hundreds of them. In every crack and crevasse of the car.

He could feel his blood pressure rising.

Someone put these in my unit. Just wait till I find out who did this. Just wait.

After several hours of surveillance, the guys headed back to the station. One by one, they filed into the captain's office to give an update of the night. When everyone had arrived, the captain debriefed the detectives and dismissed them to go home.

"Wait just one minute," the victim of Terry's prank interrupted. "Who's the dill weed that put the bag of crickets in my car?"

The guys looked around at each other, and then asked him what he was taking about.

"You know what I'm talking about. The crickets. Someone put hundreds of crickets in my car. I still can't get them all out. They drove me crazy all night. Who did it?"

The guys were laughing so hard that it was hard to pinpoint any one person who could have been guilty.

"That's a good one. I wish I'd have thought of that."

"Crickets… Man, whoever it was, that was clever."

No one would admit to the well-deserved prank, and crickets became the object of jokes for weeks,

"So who wants to go fishing Saturday? I'll buy the crickets," someone would say, and the guys would roll with laughter.

Only one person other than Terry knew who had done it. Jason Thompson and Terry were buddies. Jason made sure that Terry had been given plenty of time to unload the bag of crickets in the car just minutes before departing for the surveillance.

Terry had worked at a hardware store when he was in college that had a huge cricket cage in the back of the warehouse. Terry knew that the little critters were loud, especially when you get them in a pack, which is what he did. He had purchased a bag of them before he went to work that day.

Terry never told anyone but Jason who had been the mastermind behind the notorious prank, although all of the officers would have loved to have been the one to have thought up this great revenge. Jason did not tell anyone either, until Terry passed away.

After Terry's death, Lieutenant Hayes called Jason into his office, knowing that he was having a heard time dealing with what had happened. Consoling Jason was difficult for the lieutenant, as words at a time like that could not soothe the wounds that all of the officers felt. They sat together and reminisced about the times they had spent with Terry.

"We always had fun, at work and off duty," Jason said. "Terry and Lynn would hang out with Lauren and me, and Lauren and Lynn were becoming good friends."

"Terry was a lot of fun to be around," Hayes agreed. "I think that people really didn't realize how funny he was. I know that he was one of the new ones here and that he was a bit quiet, but when you got to know him he really had a quirky sense of humor."

"Do you remember the crickets, Lieutenant?"

"Of course, I do. Who doesn't? Wait a minute. Are you telling me that Terry was the one who did that?"

"Yep."

"I never would have guessed it. He sure had a poker face. I don't think that anyone knew it was him."

"They didn't. But it was Terry. We laughed so hard about that for a long time. I miss him, Lieutenant. My buddy is gone. We just went on a cruise together last month. I can't believe he's gone."

Lieutenant Hayes spoke at Terry's funeral about what a great a guy he was. He spoke about the person he was at work—a dedicated person, someone who cared, a team player, a person with humor and a zest for life. He told the story of the crickets. He announced that Terry was the culprit. That was the first time anyone knew who had been audacious enough to play a joke on the resident joker.

I could just hear Terry up in heaven laughing as he watched and saying, "Now, who got the last laugh?"

13

On the morning of August 10, six detectives listened as Frankie Caruso briefed them on the day's activities. Officer Neal Noel had obtained a search warrant for a duplex at 3634 Capital Heights Avenue in the mid-city area of Baton Rouge. He had already made a couple of buys from the dealer, Gergely Devai, and the unit was ready to move in and make the arrest.

"We're just going to do a knock and talk," Frankie said to the men. "This shouldn't be a big deal. Maybe we'll turn this guy into an informant."

"You want me to bring Buster just in case," Terry asked.

"Yeah, just in case," Neal responded.

Terry grabbed Buster as the men headed for their vehicles, prepared for whatever they would face. When they arrived at the residence, Jeff Pittman and Brett Busbin headed around back in case the suspect tried to escape through a window. Eric Burkett stood with Frankie at the bottom of the stairs that led to the front door. Dennis Smith and Neal Noel began knocking on the door. Terry was standing just to their right side.

"We heard music, but no one was answering the door," Frankie said. "One of the guys had heard a noise inside so we knew that someone was there. We kept knocking."

Terry was holding Buster. "You want me to go ahead and hit it?" he said. Neal answered, "Yeah."

Terry moved closer to the door and hit it with the battering ram, but it didn't open. Frankie and Eric started climbing the stairs, coming up behind Terry, Neal and Dennis.

Terry hit it again. This time, it flew open. Terry, Neal and Dennis ran inside.

Frankie heard the sounds of gunfire. *Pop, pop…pop, pop, pop.*

"I couldn't believe it," Frankie recalled. "I opened the door of my truck and took cover. I could see inside the house, and I saw Dennis fall in the doorway. Neal stumbled out and fell off the porch. I saw a guy standing inside, halfway in the doorway with his hands up."

Frankie trained his gun on the man. He could see a wound on his side and blood gushing from it. Frankie and Jeff ran up the stairs and wrestled the man to the ground. Frankie called for help.

"Officers down. I repeat. Officers down. 3634 Capital Heights Avenue."

Frankie bent down to check on Dennis and Neal. "We've got help coming," he said. "Hang in there."

Jeff, Brett and Frankie went inside to search the house, not knowing yet if the guy they had apprehended was the shooter. Then Frankie saw Terry.

"Terry! Terry!" he cried.

Terry was lying in a pool of blood on the floor. Frankie knew that he was wearing a bulletproof vest, so he was sure that he was only injured. Terry's sunglasses had come off. He told Terry that help was coming.

"We had to search the house to make sure no one else was in there. I had confidence they would be alright. My heart wasn't even pounding like it normally does. It just didn't seem real that anyone could die, especially Terry."

The three men went upstairs, but the door at the top of the stairs was closed. Frankie ran and got Buster, then threw it at the door, but it didn't open. He had Jeff cover him and forced his way in. The room was empty. Frankie realized they already had the shooter and hurried back down the stairs.

Frankie ran from Terry to Dennis to Neal, all the while praying, "Please God, don't let him be dead."

Terry looked like he was dead. There was blood under his neck and head. He had been hit in the vest and between his eyes.

"Please, God, please. Don't let him die," Frankie prayed as he bent over him.

Emergency personnel began to arrive. Dennis was lying on the ground outside having difficulty breathing. He had ducked down when the shots began and had been hit in the back. The bullet had lodged in his shoulder. Someone said to pick up his legs to help him breathe. The officers did, and Dennis's breathing returned to normal.

Neal was on the ground beside him. He had been shot in the leg.

The shooter was still on the ground where Frankie had left him. Frankie heard him say, "Can I have some water?"

Frankie looked at him with disgust. "I hope you die," he said. Frankie had no mercy to give.

A detective grabbed the shooter's arm and dragged him out of the way so that EMS personnel could attend to the fallen officers first. Frankie watched numbly. "That's good," he thought.

He walked back into the house to check on Terry.

The man working on Terry looked up. "He's gone," he said.

Frankie couldn't believe it. *He can't be gone. What will I tell Vicki? What will I tell his father? How are they going to be able to deal with this?*

Lieutenant Hayes told Frankie he needed to go back to the office.

"Y'all don't understand," Frankie said. "I have to tell Vicki and Terry. I have to tell them little Terry's gone. What are they going to do?"

Frankie couldn't leave. He was in shock. "I had an eerie feeling. All I could think was that Terry was gone. The baby I had held in my arms. The son of my friend. The man who had become my friend. The man I had promised to watch out for. He was gone."

Finally, some officers convinced Frankie to accompany them back to the station where he had to give his statement and give up his gun as is the protocol. Frankie gave the statement numbly, still in a state of shock. Every police officer is aware of the danger of the job, but no one expects that three officers will be shot in a routine drug raid. No one was prepared for the death of the young officer who had worked so hard to become a narcotics agent.

The shooter, Devai, died at the hospital. Frankie later learned that he had been sawing off a shotgun when they had knocked on the door, that he had ripped off another drug dealer and had a large quantity of marijuana growing in the upstairs room of the apartment.

Much has changed in the narcotics unit of the Baton Rouge Police Department since Terry's death. All of the officers involved were required to see psychologists to help them deal with what had happened.

"I didn't want to do that. I wanted to handle it on my own," Frankie said. "I was ready to knock on another door, to get more scum off the street."

But since Terry died, the officers no longer knock on doors when they have a warrant. "We're not so nice anymore. We hit each house tactically," Frankie explained. "We use Buster more frequently. We attach a chain to burglar bars, then to our trucks and rip them out. We pull out windows. We've learned that you never know what is waiting on the other side of that door."

Dennis Smith has been unable to return to duty as the bullet he took paralyzed his right side. On the day of the incident, Dennis was in bad shape but the chances were good that he was going to survive. A friend walked up to his father and expressed his sympathy. Dennis's father thanked the man, then said, "You know something, my son is alive. Whatever happens, we're going to handle it. But there's a family over there planning a funeral. They are the ones who need your prayers."

Neal Noel recovered from his leg wound and has returned to active duty, more determined than ever to serve his community by removing drug dealers from society.

But Terry Melancon will never return to the job he so loved.

"Since Terry died, I picture him every day in that house. Every day. My dad died in 1977, and I was the one who found him. Even today, very seldom does a week go by that I don't picture that in my mind. I know, like my dad, it's not going to go away—that image in my mind. I tear up a lot," Frankie said, tears gathering in his eyes as he spoke.

"Why did he have to die? Everything anyone said that was good about Terry was one hundred-percent true. He didn't deserve to die. He was always so happy. He was always so proud of everyone he knew—his mom and dad, his family, his church. He loved his job so much. Everyone would always tease me about Terry being 'my boy.' He was my boy. And one day I might realize why God took him, why the good guy dies and the bad people live. But right now, it's still hard for me to understand.

"I hurt a lot for Big Terry and Vicki. I can't help but think that I told her I would watch out for her son. I made that promise to her. And now he's gone."

14

Officers Gill and Schrantz, along with Detective Bryant, patrolled the area around Florida Boulevard as a team. This part of Baton Rouge was relatively quiet with only minor arrests made on a daily basis. The call they received at 3:20 that afternoon was shocking, hardly something any of them were prepared to hear.

Officers down. Repeat. Officers down.

They were patrolling only minutes away from the scene and rushed to the aid of their fellow officers. One was already gone, and the other two were fighting for their lives. Upon arrival at the scene, they noticed what appeared to be barely controlled chaos. Ambulances and fire trucks lined the street.

Officer Dennis Smith was on the ground fighting for his life. He lay there unconscious while emergency personnel worked furiously to save him.

Officer Neal Noel had been shot in the knee. The bullet had torn through his leg and shattered his kneecap. Police officers watched with tears rolling down their cheeks as Noel and Smith were carefully put on stretchers and brought to the Baton Rouge General Hospital emergency room.

Gill, Schrantz and Bryant escorted the ambulance to the hospital. They hurried the patients past the news cameras that had beaten them there. Doctors and nurses met the ambulance and rushed the officers into the emergency room. After securing the emergency room from the press, the men returned to the scene of the crime, wanting to do anything they could to help with the situation. Like the other police, their faces reflected the shock, the disbelief that this could have happened. There was no comfort to be found from the scene or from each other. Not now.

After a few minutes of questioning bystanders and commiserating with other officers, a call came over the radio—armed robbery in progress.

For the second time in less than an hour, they hit their sirens and rushed to the scene of a crime in progress. As they cautiously exited their vehicle, an officer yelled from across the street that the suspect was armed. Hearing the officer's warning, the suspect looked back at them, then began running through a nearby field.

The police gave chase. They got close enough to the robber's vehicle to see a black semi-automatic handgun in the man's right hand. The suspect tried to get into his vehicle but could not. He ran toward the front of the vehicle and then around to the other side. When he could find no avenue of escape, he raised the gun, placed his arm carefully on the hood of the car and pointed the gun directly at the officers.

He pulled the trigger.

It wouldn't fire.

He pulled it again and again, but it would not fire. Repeatedly, he tried to shoot the officers while they continued to run toward him.

The man pulled the trigger again, then shook the gun and tried clear the jam by pulling at the chamber. He pointed it directly at Gill's head and pulled the trigger. Officer Gill looked directly down the barrel of death, but the gun jammed again.

Desperate now, the gunman approached another car in the parking lot where an elderly man was seated behind the wheel waiting for his daughter to return from shopping. The gunman pulled the man from the seat of the car and got into it, gunning the engine and slamming it into reverse. The car spun in a large semicircle and stopped when it hit a large concrete embankment. The vehicle became air born, landing on the other side of the embankment. The engine killed.

Gill, Schrantz and Bryant approached the car carefully, yelling to the suspect to raise his hands and drop his weapon. They had him! They handcuffed the suspect and placed him in the backseat of their car.

After help arrived, they began to investigate what had happened. They looked inside of the car the suspect had hijacked and were shocked to see two babies strapped in car seats in the back, both crying and obviously traumatized from the incident.

As the officers carefully removed the babies from their seats, their mother ran toward the crashed car. They handed her babies to her. The man who had been pulled from the car came back as well, fearful about the condition of his grandchildren. His relief when he saw they were okay was palpable. His car was quite another thing. It had been destroyed.

The officers picked up the gun to find that it was fully loaded. The bullets had simply jammed in the chamber repeatedly. While one of their fellow officers had been killed just blocks away and two others were fighting for their lives, these lives of these officers had been spared.

The suspect was brought to jail and charged with attempted murder and carjacking. He was identified as Clifford Etienne, also known as the "Black Rhino."

Etienne had been incarcerated for armed robbery and had spent that time in prison learning to fight. Upon his release, he had devoted his life to boxing and had become a heavyweight championship contender. In 2000, he fought Mike Tyson. He lasted three minutes in that fight. But that was before drugs took over his life.

Etienne was found guilty at trial. The young man who once had the talent to fight heavyweight champions would now spend much of the rest of his life in prison.

What I have always found interesting about this is that just blocks away a fellow officer, my son, had died, and this incident could have easily taken the lives of other officers in the same afternoon. Loaded guns rarely jam. All of the officers involved in that incident knew that what happened was nothing short of a miracle. Something stopped that gun from killing those officers.

Prem Burns, the district attorney who prosecuted The Black Rhino, reported that this incident was obviously an intervention from God, a miracle on a tragic day when three officers had already been shot.

These officers knew that their lives had been spared that day. God tells us that He has appointed the day that we will die. Fortunately for their families and the community, it wasn't their day.

The officers were awarded medals of honor for their bravery during this difficult situation. They had stared down death through the barrel of a fully loaded and firing gun. They had lived to tell about it. Terry had not been so lucky.

15

As I sat in that hospital waiting for word of Terry's condition, I thought about the difficulty of being a police officer, how they never know if they will wake up the next morning, if they will be alive to watch their children grow up. Thinking about the officer who had been killed made me feel so sad for his family.

When you could be that family, you can imagine what they will have to endure. I thought about the mother, who I knew would be devastated.

God, please help her, I prayed.

I was in the habit of saying a quick prayer when I saw an ambulance passing by with its sirens on because I knew that the person in there must be very ill, so praying for the family of the officer who had died was natural for me. I couldn't imagine what a family would do with the news that their son or daughter had been killed. It was hard enough just knowing that Terry had been shot in the leg. I wondered how they would handle it. I could only imagine and pray.

Please, God, help them.

I knew better than most how hard it was to be a police officer and how difficult it was for the families who loved them. Theirs was a dangerous job that was never done. As soon as they removed one criminal from the street, another was waiting and eager to take his place. But they did it because they loved it, because they felt a sense of responsibility to keep their community safe. They were willing to die for it, and now one had. Being the mother of a policeman has always filled me with such pride, but then I felt an overwhelming sense of sadness for the other family even as I worried about Terry.

I watched as the chief of police and the mayor walked in the room. I remember thinking it was very nice of them to show such concern for Terry. I waited for them to walk over, to tell me that he was okay.

Chief LeDuff knelt down in front of me and took my hands in his. I didn't understand why he was doing that, why he had such a distressed look on his face.

"He's gone. I'm so sorry. He's gone."

I could not comprehend the reality of this. I just stared at him.

What do you mean…gone? Gone where? He was my son this morning, and now he's gone. This is so very wrong.

"What happened?" I finally managed to get out. "He was shot in the leg. What happened? Why? Why?"

"There was some misinformation," the chief explained. "It was another officer who was shot in the leg. Terry is gone."

I listened, but I could not understand what he was saying. My mind could not handle it.

I couldn't think. I couldn't breathe.

I looked around for Terry Sr. I looked for Kaylan and Lacey. They were crying.

He can't be gone. I want to see him. I want to see him just one more time.

I couldn't move.

What will we do? Where is he? What does gone mean?

I finally made my way to my husband, to my girls. We held onto each other tightly. I remember crying out with all my being, feeling like my heart had been ripped out. My precious family would never be the same without Terry.

How are we going to function without him? I need him to be here.

Terry, I need you. Please, don't leave us. Please. Please, Terry, no. My life, our lives, will never be the same.

I looked at the chief, and suddenly a peace came over me like I have never experienced. I felt it washing through me. The Bible talks about a peace that passes understanding. I did not understand it, nor was it justified, but that peace was there. I had a clear picture of where he was. I knew where Terry had gone. My Terry was in heaven. He had often talked about heaven and paradise as though it was the ultimate vacation—perfection given as a reward for goodness. My son knew that when he left this life he would go to heaven. For him, heaven was an "I can't wait to see it" reality. Terry was there. I knew it. He was with Jesus.

"This is something that I know for certain," I said to everyone in that room. "He's in heaven."

I don't remember much more about the events that took place in that hospital on that horrible day, but months later, I spoke with a woman who had been there. I didn't remember her, but she recognized me. Tearfully, she told me of the incredible peace and the presence of God in that room. She recalled me saying that Terry was in heaven, and she referred to it as a supernatural event, filled with strength, peace and prayer. Very simply, God had been there with us.

16

The sound of a solemn voice crackled across police radios throughout the city as every officer in Baton Rouge listened intently, many with tears streaming down their faces.

1258 August 10, 2005
Headquarters N440...
Headquarters N440...
Headquarters N440...
This is a final call for Detective Terry Lee Melancon Jr. of the
Baton Rouge City Police
With honor, integrity and dignity
N440
May he rest in peace.

Many officers sat in their units on the side of the road as they listened to the voice telling them that Narcotics Detective 440, Terry Melancon, would never again be called back to headquarters.

It was the official end of his watch.

He would never go back home to his family, would never play jokes again, would never arrest another drug dealer. Terry's career ended at the age of thirty-one. And even as they listened and mourned for their fellow officer and friend, every person listening to that call knew that, but by the grace of God, it could have been any one of them.

17

Terry Sr. lay beside me in bed stiff and tense, staring at the ceiling. I watched him wipe the tears in his eyes with the bed sheets. I had never seen him do that before, not in all the years I had spent loving him.

He had cried when he found out I had cancer and then again when his father passed away, but this was different. He was such a strong man, and now I watched him cry, the tears just flowing down his face with no attempt made to hide them or to be strong. There could be no strength this night. Or sleep. Whatever sleep we might have gotten was constantly interrupted by the sound of the other crying. We both tried hard not to break down completely, to sob our grief for everyone to hear.

But we couldn't do that.

That would be like admitting the truth.

Our Terry was gone.

Terry had been his father's best friend. They had loved being together. Terry respected his dad's advice. He knew that he would always be honest with him. Terry Sr. was good about directing his son about his financial future.

"Buy a house, son. That's a great investment. You can't go wrong with real estate."

Terry did just that. He bought his first house when he was twenty-six and then built his second house two years later with the proceeds from the first. His dream home—a lovely new home on a lake with large windows that took full advantage of the beautiful view. He had been so proud.

His dad had always helped him any way he could. Life would be so different for my husband without his son, his best friend.

I remember thinking that Terry was in heaven. I can't remember ever doubting that. I knew I had to hold on to that thought. It was the only thing that would get me through this. My husband could not grasp that just yet. He could not understand why God had chosen to take Terry from us.

I didn't know why either, but I knew there was a reason and that Terry's faith had been so strong. He was with God now, but that thought didn't make the fact that he was gone from us any easier.

How could this happen? My only son. I can't live without him. I don't want to live without him. He was such a good boy.

Why?

Never again would he ask me what I was cooking or play jokes on us or look out for his sisters. Never again would I get to see his beautiful face, the boy who had turned into such a wonderful young man. I buried my face in the pillow already soaked with my grief. I wondered how we get through the next few days, the rest of our lives, without him.

The next morning we stumbled from our bed to a numbing realization—we have to bury our son. Before leaving the hospital we had been instructed to meet with the funeral home director the next day. That day was here. I could not believe this was happening. I had to go to a funeral home to prepare for my son's funeral.

Lacey, Kaylan and Lynn went with us. We were ushered into a room made appropriately dark with deep brown wood paneling. A large mahogany desk sat in one corner. Several leather chairs faced the desk.

"I'm Mr. Demarcy," said the funeral director solemnly. "Please have a seat. I am so sorry for your loss."

We sat in the chairs and said nothing. Speaking did not come easily to any of us.

"Can I offer you anything to drink?"

"No thank you," someone said. I reached for one of the tissues on the desk.

"I want you to know that the funeral is being fully donated by our company, Rabenhorst Funeral Home," Mr. Demarcy said. "As a company, we want to say how much we appreciate your sacrifice, and we feel it is the least we can do."

Ever a proud man, Terry Sr. sat up straighter. "Thank you, sir, but we will gladly pay for this…"

The funeral director stopped him mid-sentence. "I could not accept a dime considering the huge sacrifice that your son made."

I watched my husband shake the man's hand with a firm appreciative grip.

"Now, I have to tell you that you may want to hold the funeral at your local church," Mr. Demarcy advised. "From what I am hearing, this funeral will attract a record crowd."

Because it was too painful to watch the news, we were unaware of the media coverage that Terry's death was receiving. My son attracting a record crowd to his funeral…it sounded a bit strange to me.

"Have you seen the news?" he went on. "This is the top story and has been since it happened. The community is devastated. I know that our facility will never be able to hold the number of people that I am assuming will come."

Unable to quite comprehend what he was saying, I called the pastor at my church and asked if we could have the funeral there. Without hesitation, he agreed.

The wake and the funeral would be held at the church Terry loved, the Healing Place Church that had brought so much to our lives. The church could hold over one thousand people, people who would come to say good-bye to my son.

"Now, we need to pick out a coffin." My stomach clenched at those words. I felt my knees weaken. I wanted to run out. I wanted to scream.

I don't think I can do this. A coffin for my son. This can't be happening.

Mr. Demarcy got up from his chair and walked to the wall. He pushed on the paneling, and it swung open to reveal a room that was brightly lit.

We got up and walked toward a variety of coffins, brightly displayed side by side.

How can this be? I can't choose a coffin for my son. I can't believe this is real.

Terry Sr. pointed to one. "How about this one?" We all immediately agreed and quickly left the room. I felt like I was going to be sick.

Next we had to choose the flowers for the top of the coffin. We chose a little shop that my husband often used to send me flowers. Mr. Demarcy called to tell them we were coming. We talked about what we wanted on the way to the shop—a large bouquet of red roses with Terry's Bible resting in the middle. He would like that.

We placed the order and waited for the bill. The flower shop would not accept any money for the enormous arrangement they planned to make. They even insisted on arranging a large bouquet for Lynn to express her love and devotion to Terry as well.

Our next appointment was the cemetery. Earlier that year, Terry Sr. and I had purchased two plots for ourselves, but we certainly never dreamed we would be in this situation. Without saying a word, we both knew we wanted Terry to be by those plots.

After choosing where Terry would be buried and talking to the director about what we should expect for that day, the director leaned forward to tell us that the gravesite was a donation from Resthaven Garden of Memories. He insisted that he could not accept any money for the huge sacrifice that our son made for our community.

We felt like we were accepting charity, something that was totally alien to us, yet everyone we had talked with had been so insistent. They hurt with us. What I didn't yet know is that the whole Baton Rouge community hurt. Our community grieved with us. Not watching the news had sheltered us from the outpouring of emotion our community was showing.

They saw the senseless killing of a young man who lived his life to serve his community and his God. They saw something special in Terry.

The news stations were bombarded with stories about the kindness this young man had showed others throughout his life. Everybody seemed to know Terry. They saw my son as a man who loved his family, who loved his fiancé, who loved what he did and who loved God. He had been unafraid to share his faith with the people he met. But most importantly, he had lived his faith. His life had been a testament to his belief in Christ.

He was a remarkable man, and yet I knew only a part of him. He touched so many people—people I did not know about until after he died. He never told anyone or boasted about the things he did. He simply helped people when no one was around to watch, people who had been changed through his kindness. He had told them that there is more to life than what we have here, that there is a God who loves them and who can help them. It wouldn't be long before I discovered just how many people Terry had touched.

On the day of the wake, we arrived at the church an hour early. We were still numb and simply going through the motions of what we had to do, each of us fearful of having to tell Terry good-bye.

We were met by the pastor and escorted into the enormous empty church. I had never been there when it was empty. It felt strange. Everything felt strange. The coffin was at the front of the church. As we made our way up the long isle toward it, I thought that I would not make it. I didn't want to see him there. I could barely keep from breaking down when I saw his body lying there dressed in his uniform that he had worn so proudly.

He looked like he was sleeping. I rubbed his hair and talked to him. For a moment, I felt like he was still here. But only for a moment. And then I wept. I wept that I would never see him smile again. He would never make me laugh again. I would never feel his hug or hear his voice. Never was incomprehensible to me.

The front row where we were to sit was lined with boxes of tissue, and bottles of water were under each chair. I wondered why I even noticed that small detail. We sat there and waited, trying to compose ourselves, occasionally just holding on to each other.

The pastor led us in a prayer, and then told us that guests were starting to arrive. Before long the Honor Guard was standing at attention on both sides of the coffin. We watched in awe as the church filled, then overflowed. Thousands of people were waiting to pay their respects to Terry. Policemen from all over Louisiana attended. Over and over, people stopped to press our hands, to hug our necks, to tell us a story about what Terry had done for them.

The funeral was held the following day. When we arrived at the church, hundreds of policeman on motorcycles and patrol cars were strategically lined up in the parking lot.

It was so difficult to walk toward the coffin again, the coffin that was now home to my son. The Honor Guard stood proudly at attention beside it as the church quickly filled.

The giant screen at the top of the stage displayed a slide show of Terry during his years on the police force. I watched as memories of my son with his family and friends flashed on the screen before me. Those pictures, those memories were now all I had left.

The slide show stopped when the funeral music started.

I Can Only Imagine was the first song. It was the perfect song.

> *I can only imagine*
> *What it will be like*
> *When I walk*
> *By your side*
> *I can only imagine*
> *What my eyes will see*
> *When your face*
> *Is before me*
> *I can only imagine.*

Terry loved that song. I knew that if he were looking down on us, he was smiling as he listened. And as people who had known him and loved him began to speak about him, I began to feel a pride in him bigger than anything I had felt before.

Laurie Daigle spoke first. She talked about living next to Terry with her husband, Jason.

Jason and Terry were childhood friends, but Laurie was the one that Terry talked to about God. They sometimes sat in their backyards and talked for hours.

Laurie spoke about the passages from the Bible that Terry loved best: *Follow me and I will make you fishers of men.* She said that she could still hear him saying that he could just see Jesus telling those disciples that they needed to follow him. Terry told her that must have been awesome. He also spoke of the passage that said, *Cast your burdens on the Lord and He will sustain you, He will never let his people be forsaken.* Laurie recalled that Terry had told her many times when she was upset or when her problems became too difficult, to cast her burdens on the Lord and forget them. "Let Jesus take care of them," he had always said.

Laurie's grandmother had passed away the week before. "You should be jealous of her," Terry had said. "She's in paradise right now. She's with Jesus. I tell Jesus that if He wanted to take me then I would be ready. I tell Him that all the time. Not my will, but your will, Lord. I'm ready."

Right before she finished talking, Laurie hesitated for a minute, then put the paper she had been reading from on the podium. She told the crowd that she felt that Terry was standing right beside her, that he wanted her to say something. He was saying to her, "Laurie, you have to tell them." She felt like he was pulling on her sleeve. She said that Terry wanted everyone to know about Jesus. "If you don't know Jesus, then ask him to come into your life," she said. "Terry is saying, 'Just do it.'"

Lacey and Kaylan were the next to speak. I knew how difficult this was for them. They spoke about what it had been like to grow up with Terry, how he had been their role model, how he had loved them and protected them. With tears in their eyes, they spoke about how their childhood had been filled with such wonderful memories of him and how hard it would to live without him. I watched my daughters tell their brother good-bye. That's the most difficult thing I've ever had to do.

Chief LeDuff was next. As he spoke, tears filled the eyes of this big, tough man who had trained my son. He was grieving the loss of his officer and friend. He spoke of how Terry had made him laugh. He recalled Terry's "cheesy" grin. He said that Terry was his own angel—that he would make sure that the police force would not forget him.

Mayor Holden spoke of Terry as an honorable law enforcer. He said the most honorable thing about Terry was that he was a Lord enforcer. He spoke of his dedication to the police force and his love for his family and his fiancé.

Pastor Dino Rizzo delivered the eulogy with love and respect. He talked about the difference one person can make in so many people's lives. I can still hear him saying that it only takes a one person to make a difference. Terry was that kind of person.

When the service concluded, the Honor Guard escorted the flag-draped coffin to the black hearse waiting outside. We were escorted to the car that would follow Terry. It took more than twenty minutes for the procession to begin. Hundreds of motorcycle policeman manned their bikes and started down the highway. Following them were police cars from all over the state, then all of the people who had known and loved Terry.

Policemen on motorcycles rode beside our car as well as the car that carried Terry. When we turned onto the highway leaving the church, we noticed that hundreds of people had lined the streets to show their respect. It was the middle of August, and these people were standing in one hundred-degree heat to watch Terry go by. Our family was overcome with emotion at this wonderful outpouring of respect.

We noticed one little girl and her mother holding a handmade sign that read, "Thank you, Mr. Policeman." She must have been eight years old or younger. I thought about that little girl on the way to the cemetery, how her mother must have felt that she was teaching her daughter that police officers sometimes put their lives on the line, even die, to keep little girls safe.

As we turned onto the street where the cemetery was located, we noticed two huge fire trucks with both arms raised to their full range, blocking all six lanes of traffic. A gigantic American flag spread between them. That sight was incredible to us. They had done this for our Terry. We were shocked by the outpouring of love Terry received from our community. We felt so humbled. We felt that Terry would have been so proud. We were proud for him.

Bagpipes at the gravesite solemnly played *Amazing Grace* before a twenty-one gun salute ended the ceremony. Our Terry, who had been laughing and joking with us only days before, was buried. I couldn't bear to watch as the final shovel of dirt covered him.

A patrol car parked in our driveway for weeks. Both city police and state troopers took shifts parking there to show their respect. Several times over the following weeks, a helicopter would circle our property, letting us know they were there for us.

During that time, we experienced the brotherhood of the police force and what it meant to be one of them. We were included in that family.

Terry's funeral was aired nine times on television during the following month. A friend at one of the local stations told me that never before had a funeral been requested so many times. She attributed it to the remarkable man that he was.

The director at the funeral home later told us that Terry's funeral was the largest in Baton Rouge's history, topping all dignitaries, even Huey Long. Never had Baton Rouge seen such an outpouring of sympathy.

I could see now that God did not take Terry. He chose him, and even in death, Terry is still touching people here on earth.

My son. My hero.

After he had been on the police force for several years, Terry had started sending applications to The Drug Enforcement Agency (DEA), the agency he had admired since the beginning of his career.

He had been interviewed and invited to go through all the testing and physicals that were required. Terry never received an official acceptance letter, but he had been encouraged by the attitudes of those who interviewed him.

After passing the tests and the physical, he had been preparing for his last meeting with the director, who at that time would accept or deny his entrance into the agency.

One night while on a drug raid, the DEA agency was called out to assist Terry's squad. The DEA agent who Terry was going to meet for the final interview two days later went along for the ride. The agent and Terry looked at each other, and Terry smiled. The agent gave Terry a wink and a nod, letting him know that he had nothing to worry about.

Terry had been so excited. He had called us to tell us what happened. He told us that the look the agent had given him was a confirmation that he had been hired. He knew it. He had accomplished his dream.

Terry never made it to that last interview. He was killed the next day. At the funeral, the director presented us with a pin that bore the DEA designation. Terry was buried with that pin. He had accomplished his goal. I had always known that he would.

18

No one was prepared for the destruction that Hurricane Katrina unleashed on the city of New Orleans on August 29, just nineteen days after Terry passed away. Most residents were displaced to other parts of the country as their homes were destroyed and the lack of operational businesses made finding work nearly impossible, at least before the reconstruction began.

Lynn and her family were among the displaced. The hospital in which she worked was located in one of the hardest hit areas of the city, and Lynn found herself homeless and without a job like so many others. Lynn moved into Terry's house and soon found employment at Woman's Hospital in Baton Rouge as a surgical nurse. But when she discovered her mother needed surgery, she could not leave work to be at her side since her position was so new. She was worried about her mom and called the night before the operation.

"Mom, are you going to be okay?"

"Oh yeah, baby," Gaynell drawled comfortingly in her familiar New Orleans accent. "Don't you worry about me."

"But Mom, I can't get off work."

"Lynn, I'm gonna be fine. Just don't you worry, ya hear?"

"I can't help it. I love you, Mom. Call me when you get back in your room and tell Dad to call me when you get out of surgery. Okay?"

"Sure, I'll tell your dad, and I'll talk to you tomorrow."

Still, Lynn fretted.

"Mom, now say a prayer before you go in. Promise me you'll say a prayer. I'm going to be praying for you, too."

"Okay, baby, now let me go get some rest. Love you."

In her condition, Gaynell could not travel, so she was admitted to a hospital right outside of New Orleans for the procedure she needed, although she would have preferred to have Lynn attend her throughout the surgery. Lynn knew many of the nurses who worked there since they, too, had left Chalmette for employment.

Lynn felt helpless. She knew all too well the dangers of surgery. Normally, there was something she could do, some comfort she could give, but this time she could do nothing but pray.

Dear God, please take care of my mother. She has been through so much. Just please be with her. And Terry, I really need you to look after her for me. I love you, Terry. I miss you so much.

The following morning, Lynn had to drag herself to work. She forced herself to concentrate and tried not think about her mother being in surgery.

Around noon, she got the call for which she had been waiting all morning.

"Hey, Mom, are you okay?"

Still sounding little groggy, Gaynell said softly, "Yeah, baby, everything went fine. And I think your angel, Terry, was watching over me. In fact, I know he was."

"What are you talking about, Mom?"

"I'm talking about Terry. He was with me—watching out for me."

"How do you know?" Lynn asked, thinking maybe her mom was still suffering from the aftereffects of the anesthesia.

"When I got back into my room after the surgery, I noticed a dry erase board on the wall—you know, one of those boards that you write on with a marker and it wipes clean."

"I know what that is, but what happened?"

"Well, T.L. Melancon was written on the board. I thought I was dreaming when I saw that until I noticed a lady entering my room. I asked her who T.L. Melancon was and she told me that was her name. She told me that she was my nurse. I asked her what the T.L. stood for, and she said, Terri Lee."

Lynn sat listening quietly, barely breathing.

"I made her repeat her name several times. She kept saying, 'Terri Lee Melancon,' only she spelled Terri with an i."

Lynn found her voice. "Are you sure that was her name?"

"Yes, Lynn, that was her name. Your boy was looking out for me, that's for sure."

"Mom, did you know that Lee is Terry's middle name?"

"What I know is that God sent an angel to take care of me. I know that," Gaynell said.

Lynn went over and over the conversation after she hung up the phone. She called me the next day with so much excitement in her voice she could hardly contain herself. She told me the story that her mother had told her.

I couldn't believe it.

"What are the odds that your mother's nurse would have Terry's name? Why don't you try to call the hospital later and see if you can talk her?"

"That's a good idea," Lynn responded. "I want to tell her this story."

Later that day, Lynn called the hospital, hoping to get in touch with the nurse who had Terry's name.

"This is Lynn Harwell. My mother was a patient on your floor yesterday. She was released this morning. I was wondering if I could talk to her nurse, Terri Melancon."

"Terri isn't here today," the receptionist said. "She's a traveling nurse, and she was only here for that day. Were she and your mother good friends?"

"No, they had not met before."

"You're kidding, right?"

"No. Why?"

"Because Ms. Melancon and your mother talked like they had known each other for years. Ms. Melancon hardly left her side. I can't believe that they had never met."

We never did find Nurse Melancon, but both Lynn and I knew with a certainty that God had answered Lynn's prayer. Word for word. He had sent Terri Lee Melancon to watch over Gaynell through her ordeal.

Although I struggled with Terry's death, moments like these reminded me that he was still with us all, that all I had to do was watch for the signs of his presence in our lives.

19

When I was young, the common thread in all of our Bible classes was the importance of memorizing scripture and keeping it close to our hearts. One of the first scriptures I memorized was John 3:16—"For God so loved the world that he gave his only begotten son that whosoever shall believe in Him shall not perish but have eternal life." I loved that it was so simple—that there is no magic wand, that it's not about just doing good. It's simply asking for forgiveness for my sins and believing in Jesus.

I was so proud of my newly memorized passage. God must have been proud of me, too, because it seemed that I would see 3:16 everywhere and in the most unusual places.

Often, I would wake up in the middle of the night, and it would be 3:16 in the morning. I would see it in addresses and phone numbers. It would frequently pop up unexpectedly at strange times. Whenever I saw it, I was reminded of my special passage, and I began to think that is was a private joke between me and God. For me, it was always a special moment.

I believe that God is ever attentive to the smallest details and that it is up to us to identify these gentle reminders and recognize them as more than mere coincidence. Miracles occur every day, but I think the majority of people see them as luck or good fortune or even karma.

But when I saw the death certificate and looked for the exact time of Terry's death, I gasped. Terry had died at 3:16 in the afternoon. This was no coincidence. I knew the minute I saw it that it was something that God had orchestrated. He chose to touch my heart with the sweet sign that had always been our way of communicating. He knew how much that would touch me. He chose to take my son the same way that He gave His son. He was letting me know that He had given my son eternal life. He was giving me the gifts of insight and strength. And that passage became the gift that kept on giving.

Months later, Lynn and I were among three hundred thousand women who attended a wholesale jewelry show held in Baton Rouge. This event was normally held in New Orleans, but the aftermath of Hurricane Katrina had forced a change of venue to our city.

Cars filled with women heading for the show stopped traffic on Interstate 10 for hours before the doors opened. The building chosen to host the show was much smaller than is normal for events of this type, so what ensued was very chaotic. By the time the doors opened, the fire marshal was outside limiting the number of people entering the building.

Inside, there were rows and rows of vendors selling thousands of products.

Lynn and I had a great time, laughing and talking as we made our way through the crowd. We agreed that Terry would never be in this mad house. Apparently, we were wrong.

Before long, Lynn ran into a friend she had worked with in New Orleans, and we stopped to chat. Throughout the course of the day, we ran into the same girl repeatedly as we wandered about looking at the sparkling jewelry. The last time, Lynn's friend told her that she wanted to give her a Christmas present as she was going back to New Orleans and would not see Lynn again before Christmas.

The present was a precious silver bracelet, with words engraved on the inside. Lynn began to read the delicately engraved words, and then turned to me in surprise.

"Mrs. Vicki, this has John 3:16 engraved on it."

We both stared at it for a moment, and then started laughing. We had been wrong. Terry was there after all.

We talked about the odds of that bracelet being chosen for Lynn out of all of the jewelry in that show. I asked her friend where she had found it, and she pointed down a row of about three hundred vendors. "Somewhere down this aisle," she said.

It looked impossible, but Lynn and I set out to find another bracelet for me. We searched and searched until we were exhausted. It became evident that we were never going to find it. The place was so big, and there were people standing shoulder to shoulder waiting to see the items on display in the vendor's booths. Three hours later, I decided that I was not meant to have one. As we left, I did my best to hide my disappointment.

The next Monday, everyone at work who had attended the show gathered around to admire each other's finds. As we ooh-ed and aah-ed, one of my dear friends, Amy, said that she had found something at the show and felt like she had to buy it for me even though it was not yet Christmas. She said she saw it and thought of me.

It was the bracelet that Lynn and I had searched for on Saturday. It was my John 3:16 bracelet.

I started to cry, and she wondered if she had offended me.

I told her that she did not realize that God had chosen her to find the bracelet that I so desperately wanted. It meant so much more to me receiving it this way. Finding it at the jewelry show would have been nice, but receiving it this way left no doubt that God's hand was involved. Even though she had no idea about my relationship with that passage and how special it was to me, God had used her to bless me.

20

Grace and Amelia, Terry's nieces, could always bring a smile to his face. They were his pride and joy. Lacey was probably a big reason why they were so important to him. He loved Lacey so much, and he loved seeing the world though the eyes or her children.

When Gracie was born, she was the first grandchild on our side of the family. Terry was very excited, like he had been when Kaylan was born. He had loved being around her and making her happy. The same was true with Grace and Amelia, and the feeling was reciprocated. Grace loved her uncle "Tey," whose days off would usually be spent hanging out with his friend, Jimmy. First, the two men would work out, then go pig out at a buffet somewhere, and then they would hurry to visit the babies.

Gracie was an incredible little girl. She had become a big sister when she was only eleven months old. Amelia was a sweet child, but I wondered how Gracie would welcome a new baby at such a young age.

Seeing her with Amelia was amazing. She loved her and cared for her. When Amelia cried, she was truly concerned, and the older Gracie became, the more protective she became. When Amelia wanted a certain toy, Gracie would give it to her just to make her sister happy. She would get close to her face and kiss her and hold her, even at the tender age of fifteen months.

As they grew into toddlers, Amelia learned how to behave though her big sister. She learned about kindness and caring. Before meals, they would always insist on saying a prayer. We had to hold their hands, and our eyes had better be closed just like theirs. They usually peeked to make sure everyone was being truly prayerful and had their eyes closed.

One Thanksgiving day, just before the dinner meal, our family stood around the living room and held hands to say our Thanksgiving prayer. The room was filled with several dozen friends and relatives, and the kids stood in the middle wondering when they could eat. At the end of our prayer to thank God for our many blessings, my dad said in a slightly raised voice, "Amen," which prompted Gracie to shout, "Go Tigers!" The room erupted in laughter, and Gracie ran to hide by her mother, embarrassed about her untimely response.

But Gracie and Amelia were special. I saw something in their hearts at a very young age that sparkled with the love of God.

I attribute a lot of this behavior to their parents. Lacey and Craig were incredible parents. They loved them so much and made sure that their finances allowed Lacey to stay home with them. It was a blessing and also a sacrifice that they both chose to make.

When the girls were ages two and three, they were so much fun. Amelia was a little pistol. She weighed twenty-two pounds by the time she was two.

Terry would tease her and say, "Amelia, what's that hanging from your shorts? Are they strings? No. Wait a minute. That's your legs."

Amelia would laugh, not getting the joke at all, but laughing at the laughter that it always aroused.

"Why are you so cute, Amelia?" Terry would ask, and she would smile that shy little smile that always made him melt.

When Terry died, Grace and Amelia were too young to understand what had happened. They would see pictures of Terry and smile, but never questioned where he might be. Fortunately, Craig's parents took care of the girls during the funeral, so they were not exposed to the tremendous amount of sorrow that was present there. So one day when Lacey wanted to visit Terry's gravesite, she felt it unnecessary to tell the girls where she was going.

She was meeting me for lunch that day and was a little early. She had decided to stop by the grave, clean off the grave marker and spend a few minutes talking to her brother. She parked close to the site so that she could keep an eye on the girls as they watched a video. When she was finished, she got back in the van and started to drive off. In her rear view mirror, Lacey noticed that Gracie had turned around in her car seat and was saying something. She could hear her saying, "Bye, Tey Tey."

"Gracie, what did you just say?"

"I told Uncle Tey Tey bye bye."

"What do you mean, Gracie? Who are you talking to? Where was Tey Tey?"

"Uncle Tey Tey was right there, Mommy. I told him bye," she said, pointing to the gravesite.

"Mommy, Tey Tey had a boo-boo, and it falled off."

Lacey knew that Gracie had not been there before. She knew her child could not have known where they were. But she listened as Gracie told her what she had seen and believed that she had seen someone.

"Gracie, where was Tey Tey's boo-boo? Tell me, where did you see his boo-boo?"

"It was in Jesus's hands, Mommy. His boo-boo was in Jesus's hands. Tey Tey was standing by Jesus, and his boo-boo was in Jesus's hands. Jesus took them away."

Lacey listened, stunned. "What else happened, Gracie?"

"Tey Tey gave me a big hug," she said, demonstrating for Lacey by wrapping her arms around her waist, closing her eyes and squeezing tight.

Realizing the significance of what her daughter had just told her, Lacey began to smile. Terry was okay. He was standing by Jesus, and he had no more boo-boos. He was whole and in the hands of the almighty God.

The date was 3-16-2006. Once again, God had given us a sign to keep us strong. This time, it had come from the mouth of a babe.

21

The Baton Rouge community had been devastated by the news that such a young officer had been killed. Everyone wanted to help. Accounts were set up at local banks for the outpouring of contributions that people felt moved to give. They hurt for us. They hurt for themselves.

We received thousands of cards and flowers from so many people we did not know. It took me by surprise that this event, the death of my son, was such a tragedy for others. Local television and radio stations graciously orchestrated the effort to help people cope and to reassure us that our community loved and supported us.

And then three weeks after the funeral, Hurricane Katrina wreaked her tremendous fury to change all of our lives once again. We lived ninety miles from where the center of the storm hit, and most of our family and friends were forced to evacuate. Terry's newly built home suddenly became a shelter for all of his loved ones. Three families lived there for several months while they tried to find missing relatives who had scattered across the South. Because phone lines were down for weeks, communication was virtually impossible. All of the evacuees would later learn that they had lost their homes.

Lynn's family had lived in their home in Chalmette for more than forty years, and now it was gone, with not even a photograph left behind. Her mother's sister and her daughter had nowhere to go, so they came to us. Lynn's two brothers and their families were also homeless and stayed there. Terry's house soon filled with blow-up mattresses used for makeshift beds. Everyone made call after call to shelter after shelter trying to locate loved ones that were missing.

Mike and Sheri Melancon, my brother and sister-in-law, lost two homes. The storm cut through the center of their family home and a summer home they owned on the Mississippi Gulf Coast. Katrina destroyed them both. They, too, were suddenly homeless and stayed with us for a while.

It was reported by the news that one out of every two households in the Baton Rouge area had evacuees living in them. Everyone I talked with knew someone who was homeless because of Katrina.

So when a gentleman from a local bank called to tell us that he had a check for us—donations from our generous community—the decision to use that money to help our Katrina victims was easy. We helped those who needed it the most. It struck me that even after his death, Terry was still helping people.

Then our pastor called one day to inquire if we had set up a foundation in Terry's memory. I told him that we felt like the money we collected needed to go to the victims of Hurricane Katrina. I said that if he wanted to make a contribution, he might consider donating to worldwide missions, which was something that Terry would have wanted.

Several months later, our church asked if my family would mind being interviewed for a special presentation to be shown during Easter services.

We met at the church for the interview. The stage was beautifully decorated with a huge life-size wooden cross lying on its side. The platform was situated in the middle of the church so that the cross would be visible for the cameras. Emily Morrow, the interviewer, carefully asked each of us how Terry had impacted our lives. She wanted to know what kind of man he was, how he had touched people.

We told her how incredible his life had been. We recalled stories that had been relayed to us after his death about the acts of kindness to others that he had hidden from us. We talked about our love for him and how much we missed him. We expressed our belief that God had chosen Terry to help change lives by showing them Christ through him.

Easter service was held at the Baton Rouge River Center downtown. Nearly four thousand people attended. It was an incredible service. The Christian band, The Katina's, shared with us their incredible musical talent. Midway through the service, the interview was played for the audience. Pastor Dino spoke about how one person can change so many lives. He said that it just takes one person, that we can all be that one person.

After he had spoken for several minutes about how important our job is to reach those people who don't know how to get to heaven, he looked at my family and said that the Healing Place Church had recently purchased a piece of property in Mozambique, Africa. This city in Africa was one of the most impoverished areas, with the HIV virus having infected approximately one out of every two people there. Many families live under trees with little or no means of survival.

He informed us that the church's mission was to build a chapel there.

"The chapel will be named The Terry Melancon Chapel," he said.

I could not believe it. My son. A Baton Rouge police officer. Gracie and Amelia's Uncle Tey Tey. An everyday guy who simply did the right things through his life will have a church in Africa named after him. Terry's church would give people hope. I was stunned.

No greater honor could ever have been given to my family. We felt so humbled by this. We were speechless.

Several months passed —months spent grieving and trying very hard to rebuild our lives. Then one day, during another Sunday service, Pastor Dino showed the congregation pictures of the construction progress. We saw cinder blocks and a concrete floor.

The church had decided to host a dedication of the chapel that would be held the next week. More than six hundred people walked to the chapel from all over Mozambique to attend the ceremony.

I know that this church in such a far away place is going to make an unbelievable contribution to the people there, people with little hope who can now know that God loves them and that they are special. I can imagine that the ministers there will teach them about heaven and how it is the most wonderful place they could imagine.

A church in Africa. Named for Terry. Incredible.

22

It's two o'clock in the morning, and I lay awake wishing that I could tell Terry how much I love him. I think about all the things I would have wanted to do differently, about the things that I wanted to do with him but never got the chance. My life is consumed with everyday chores. I realize they are meaningless now. But I am grateful for the repetition, for the monotony, for the busy days that keep my mind occupied.

Why didn't I tell him how important he was to me? Did he know? I tell myself that he did, but it pains me to think that one moment passed by when I could have done something for him and may have missed the opportunity. It haunts me, especially at night when the house is dark and quiet and everyone is asleep. Or are they? I worry about how Terry's death has affected my children, my husband.

I remember one of the last conversations we had. Terry was trying to make an important decision about his job. He couldn't decide if he should take another position or stay where he was. There were definite pros and cons for both sides. The only advice I could give him was to give it to God. He is the only one who knows our future. I told him that if he prayed before he made the decision, God would lead him in the direction he needed to go. I said that he had to trust that his decision was the right one. That day was a lesson for us in trusting God to lead our lives.

Shortly after that conversation, Terry passed away. I miss our talks. I miss his humor. I miss him being here. It's sometimes so hard to think about that I force it to the back of my mind just to be able to function. How could someone do this to my son?

Before writing this book, I could not tell you the name of the man who shot him. To me, he is still nameless and faceless. I have no emotion for him. I don't want to waste a thought on him. He is not worth my anger.

I do pity his family, though. His mother has to endure the shame that her son brought to her family. Sometimes I think about the horror of having to live with the fact that her son could commit such a crime against someone that he did not even know—my son. How could he? And more importantly, why did he do this? Late at night I often find myself asking why.

Why was Terry the first officer to enter the house that day?

Why did the killer sit there waiting to shoot someone?

Why does it hurt so badly?

A passage from Luke is inscribed on Terry's grave marker that reads, "No greater love has one than this—that he lay down his life for his friends."

Terry did not choose to die, but he was willing to accept God's will in his life. He would always say that he wanted God's will, not his, and I know that God's will was done. I know now that God's will was to impact a community.

It has been more than a year since Terry entered heaven. Recently, someone came to me and mentioned how devastating it must have been for me that my son was murdered.

The word, "murdered" stopped me in my tracks.

Terry was murdered. I know that he died, but I had never used that word before. God had given me a totally different picture in my mind. He had painted a picture of heaven. He had sheltered me and had given me the strength to know that although Terry was not here, he was on his ultimate vacation with Jesus.

The world seems to dwell on the circumstances. I survive in the reality of my truth.

I hope sleep comes soon. Some nights I stay awake all night, squeezing my eyes shut, hoping that if I stay like that long enough, sleep will come. But other nights I sleep like a baby, exhausted from my nights spent so restlessly.

The days seem to be easier. There are distractions on which I can focus my mind. I find myself carefully planning each day so that there is little or no time with nothing to do. It helps me to stay busy, even if I'm simply reading or meditating on God's word. That always calms me. It brings peace to me.

I find myself praying that no other mother will ever have to live the pain that I have had to endure—that feeling of your heart being ripped out and that you will never get it back. No mother should have to bury her son due to a senseless selfish act of murder.

If the man who did this had known Terry, he would not have killed him. I know that in my heart. To know Terry was to know the spirit of Jesus. That killer simply planned to kill someone that day. My son was the victim of his senseless rage against society, his hate for policemen. Terry was just a random target, a blue uniform to extinguish.

My consolation is that Terry died honorably. He believed in righteousness and good. He believed in a world where his precious little nieces could live safely, protected from an underworld filled with drugs and murder. He believed in his responsibility to serve and protect. He took that very seriously. It makes me so proud to know that he died with such dignity and respect. His watch here on earth might have ended, but his watch in heaven began that day.

I often think about the passage on Terry's grave. Terry laid down his life. He had no fear on the job even though he was very aware of the danger he faced every day. He didn't dwell on the idea that being killed was something real. He focused his life on living.

His neighbor, Laurie, often talked to him about the dangers of his job, and over and over again he told her, "What's to be scared of? If it's my time to go then I will accept that. I'll be in heaven. What's so bad about that?"

Terry spoke of that place called heaven with such excitement that one would have thought he had a personal insight into how wonderful it was. Maybe he did. All I know is that he looked forward to seeing this place that God had prepared for him—especially for him—just like he has prepared heaven for all of us, custom made to fit our most wonderful dreams.

I hold on to this when I am being drawn down into haunting thoughts of his death. I try to hold on to the fact that Terry is, as some would say, in a much better place. That seems a little understated to me, but until I get there, I will never be able to comprehend the grandness of this place.

I do know that my greatest moment will be when I see my son again. He will be there waiting for me. He will open his arms, and I will run as fast as I can to greet him. I want to see his wonderful smile. I want him to embrace me and hug me tight. I want him to show me what he has experienced and to walk through heaven meeting the people that he has met. I want him to be with me when Jesus asks me what have I've done for Him. Jesus. The one who gave me the strength to endure all that life held for me.

I pray that my response will be acceptable to Him. I will tell Him that I had used the opportunities that He gave me to tell others about Him. I will thank Him for creating those opportunities for me. Obstacles and heartache, such as getting cancer and the death of my only son, taught me to place my faith in Jesus. As much as those things hurt, I know that Jesus was creating in me the ability to show others what God's strength can do for someone.

I understand that Jesus allowed my son to die so that other people could be reached through him. I know that Terry was a willing servant. God chose him. I can see what his death has done for so many people, even reaching as far away as a remote village in Africa whose people suffer horribly from poverty and disease. Terry gives them hope, the hope of Jesus.

I do feel Terry around me sometimes, and I know that he would not want any of us to be sad. I know that he did not suffer in his death. The Bible says to be absent from the body is to be present with the Lord. That day, at 3:16 in the afternoon on August 10, 2005, my son met Jesus face to face.

That day was just a normal day in his life and was not met with fear. I don't have to wonder where my son is. Jesus has allowed us to know because we knew what kind of person Terry was.

I can just imagine Jesus asking him, "Terry, did you love me when you were on earth? What did you do for me? Did you help people? Did you show them love and tell them about me?"

Terry would have answered, "Yes, every opportunity I got. I knew that one day I would see you, and I lived my life guarding my words and actions so I would not offend you. I love you, Jesus. I have since I was a little boy.

"I remember when you stood over my bed when I was young and told me not to worry, that my bad nightmares would go away. You said that I would not have to worry about them anymore, and I wasn't scared when you came to me, although most people didn't believe me when I told them. They thought that I was just dreaming, but I knew, and you did what you promised. You stopped the nightmares.

"Jesus, all throughout my life I have depended on your strength, and you were there. I know that it was because of you that I was not as hurt as I could have been when I flipped my three-wheeler as a young boy. I felt your hand under me. I told my mom and she believed me, but others wouldn't understand. But I knew that it was you. I felt your hand under my body shielding me from the concrete and gravel. I knew what it was. Thank you, Jesus.

"I remember when I was awakened one night by your voice and heard you say to write this down. I knew that it was you. I remember writing words until they came no more. I remember going back to sleep, and you woke me up again. Again, you gave me words. All I had to write on were the bank envelopes that were in the nightstand beside my bed. I remember reading the words the next morning and being astounded by the beautiful poem that you gave me. Stuff like that is deep, and I know that some people thought that I was dreaming, but I know that I wasn't. I remember the words like they were just written."

You are my angel, my angel of light
Like the stars up above, you shine through the night
Whenever I am scared you come to the fight
You are my angel, my angel of light
Angels come to the light when their time is needed
As they go to the light, their presence is greeted
Angels in the dark, angels in the light,
Angels all around us with only heaven in sight

The time has come
They say the time has come to see the ghost
The holy one indeed because he loves you the most
My deed is done here
Pass this word around that God is looking upon us
With not a smile but a frown
Listen to the Lord like he always says
For the time has come upon us for Him to make His ways.

Terry wrote this poem about six months before he passed away. After burying him, Lynn went to his house to get his two cats, Bubba and Baby. She felt that there was something that she needed to get there in addition to the cats, but didn't know what was tugging at her heart.

As she stood in the kitchen, she looked around at the cabinets, and her eyes focused on a top cabinet in the corner. She opened it and saw nothing. She pulled up a stool to get a better look and saw papers and some envelopes.

At first glace, they looked like they only had been scribbled on by Terry. His handwriting was very identifiable. But as she looked at it closer, she recognized it to be the poem that Terry had told her about several months before.

This wasn't a dream. It was real. He actually heard from God and had written it down.

Carefully she read every word, realizing that God was speaking to us as well as Terry.

Terry was in heaven. Angels were with him. His deed here was done. It all made sense. It was what God wanted us to find at the perfect time. Peace—our peace that Terry was where God wanted him. With Him.

Several weeks after the funeral, Chief LeDuff asked if he could come to my office to give me the last of the personal items that were in Terry's desk. I told the chief about the poem and asked if he would like a copy.

By now, I had made a bunch of copies and carried them with me at all times. I gave the poem to everyone who knew Terry and many who didn't. It touched everyone who read it. I asked the chief if I could read it to him as reading it always gave me comfort.

He leaned back in the big chair with his arms slightly folded, carefully listening to every word. By the time I finished the poem, he had moved closer to me and was looking at me intently through tear-filled eyes.

"You know, our boy is watching us. It's almost funny. Mrs. Vicki," he said, "I have to tell you a story:

"When I had to make the terrible announcement to the press that your son had passed away, it was so hard for me. As policemen, we always refer to officers who have died in the line of duty as 'fallen heroes.' In fact, that was what was in my notes that I was supposed to read at the briefing. But when I got up there to speak, I referred to Terry as an angel. Until now, I didn't know where that came from. Now I know."

Chief LeDuff proved himself to be a source of strength, as well as a friend, to our family. He was not a fair-weather politician, but a caring man who supported us long after the media was silenced.

And moments like those were the ones from which I drew my strength. But I am not always so strong. And when I have my moments of weakness, it seems that Terry is always watching and waiting to pull me through. I cannot count how many times that, as Terry Sr. and I have been leaving our son's gravesite after a particularly hard visit, the song, *I Can Only Imagine* has come on the radio. It's almost like Terry is always reminding me that he is okay. And there are others who are always there to pick me up as well—my family, my friends, my pastor, and Lynn.

On one particularly bad day, Lynn called out of the blue to tell me that she felt that she needed to tell me how much Terry loved me. I have to wonder if Terry saw my tears and gently tugged at Lynn's heart to call me with the sweetest of words—"Mom, I love you."

As I answered the phone, I tried to hide the fact that I had been crying. When she asked how I was doing. I assured her that I was okay, but she didn't believe me.

"Are you sure you're okay?" she asked again.

"Well, I am having a bad day," I admitted. "Just missing him, Lynn. I want to tell him I love him. I want him to know that. I know he does, but I can't remember the last time I said it. I want to hug him. I want to feel him come up behind me and give me a big hug like he used to. I miss him so much it hurts."

I felt bad for crying to her, knowing as I did how she suffered.

"I knew something had to be wrong, Mrs. Vicki," she said.

"How did you know that?"

"I just felt like I had to call you and tell you that Terry loves you. The feeling was so strong. I thought that you might think I'm a little crazy, but I see now that Terry was trying to tell me that you needed to hear it. He wanted me to tell you that he loves you. He knew that you were missing him. Mrs. Vicki, I have never done this before, but trust me, Terry wanted me to tell you that he loves you."

What a wonderful feeling to know that God loves me so much that he would allow me to hear those words one more time.

Lynn admitted later that she felt a little odd that she had called to tell me that and had wondered how I would respond. Little had she known that I had been sitting home with picture albums, crying and sinking deeper and deeper into the very sad and lonely place that has become my companion. I am convinced that Terry had Lynn call with that message for me.

Terry is with us. I just know it. Sometimes I can feel him so close to me. But in lonelier times, I have learned to depend on the strength of God and those who love me.

All throughout Terry's life he depended on Jesus's strength. He had felt Him, and at times he experienced the vision of a heavenly angel that was sent to comfort a frightened little boy. He knew that Jesus was real and not something abstract. He knew it as fact.

I can hear Terry saying, "I love you, Jesus." And Jesus replying, "Well done, my good and faithful servant. Welcome. Come in and see what I have for you."

Terry, I know I will see you again. I know you are waiting for me in heaven. I can't wait to tell you how much you mean to me and how much we have missed you, how much we love you.

I pray that God shields Terry from seeing my tears. I don't want him to be burdened. I want him to go through heaven with wonderful thoughts.

I'll see you there, my precious son.
I'll see you in heaven.
Watch for me.

Tributes

Terry,

My son, there is not a day or a moment that goes by that I don't miss you being here with us. I have lost my best friend. I miss our talks and just being with you. We could do nothing and have fun. I thank God that you showed us where you are—in heaven. I will see you there one day. Help us here to have strength to live without you on this earth. I know you are around us. I can only imagine that you saw me in the woods hunting last weekend and heard me talking to you. What a surprise it was to see three of the biggest deer I've ever seen walking past my chair. I can only laugh to think you orchestrated that scene. I have been hunting for more than forty years and never has that happened before. Thank you, buddy. I love you. I know that you knew that. You are my only son, and I will always love you and appreciate your sacrifice. Be with me.—Dad

Terry,

Your unbelievable courage and determination to succeed and, most of all, your unwavering faith has and will continue to make my life better. Thank you for your sacrifice. I miss you every day, and I love you so much.—Lacey

Terry,

I look at you as a son. I have such respect and gratitude for what you gave for me and the police force. It was my pleasure to train you and get to know you. Your humor and dedication to whatever you did gave me a sense of pride. You have changed the voice of the police force today. My job is to never allow your memory and what you stood for leave the memories of all the men who go after you. I hope and pray that the legacy of your integrity and dedication to your faith, your family and your job will be the motto of every policeman on this force today.—Jeff LeDuff, chief of police, Baton Rouge Police Department

Terry made me realize that you can go through life and deal with it—that you don't have to let it get you down. That smile of his was always there. He made me want to be more like that. He made me a better person, for sure. He made a lot of people better.

He treated the people we arrested a step better than he had to and went out of his way to help people. He was just a good guy.—Frankie Caruso, Baton Rouge Police Department

Terry,

One year ago, you, Dennis and I stood together on the steps in front of a door that would forever change our lives. On that day, you saved our lives. You sacrificed for your brothers. You gave us time to react, and for that, there are not enough words of thanks. "No greater love has a man than this—that he lay down his life for his friends." Brother, you are that man. On that day, Dennis and I would leave without you. Only by your courage and the grace of God were we able to return to our beloved wives and children. One day, Dennis will be well enough to join me to continue the mission, but it will never be the same. Go with God and walk with the angels. Thank you, my brother.—Neal Noel, Baton Rouge Police Department

Terry,

Well, my brother, it hasn't been long and our journey continues even though we are in separate places. You left a lasting impression on all who came into contact with you through your motto, "What's your purpose?" I was blessed to have known you and often wonder what my plan holds. I do know that wherever life takes me, your memory will always help guide me. I dream of the day that my children can truly understand your sacrifice. They will, as I do, respect all that you died for. I remember my last words to you, my last sight of you, right before we entered that door that forever changed my life. I wonder what it will be like when we meet for all eternity. I only know that it will be grand and full of joy. I love you.—Dennis Smith, Baton Rouge Police Department

In giving his life for his community, Terry Melancon lived true to his dream—with determination to fight for justice and protect what is finest in life, however great the personal cost. August the tenth will be etched in our collective memory forever.—Prem Burns, assistant district attorney, East Baton Rouge Parish

Terry had the God-given ability to light up a room when he entered. Even the most serious, no-nonsense people laughed when he delivered his one-liners. His practical jokes were legendary to his family and friends. It was always obvious within our family how much this oldest grandchild was loved and respected. If I had but one child, I would want that child to mirror the honesty, integrity and ability that came so naturally to Terry.

He was a police officer who truly loved his job and felt that he was placed on this earth to serve and protect others. I regret that it took this

great loss for me to recognize the risk and sacrifice that police officers all over the world face each day to protect the lives of all of us.

Terry, you will be in our hearts and souls forever, and I look forward to seeing you again. —Laurie Schaumburger (Aunt Laurie)

I can't put into words how knowing Terry has changed the rest of my life. Terry lived every day with purpose and appreciated the smallest things that came with each day. He chose to see God's hand in everything and trusted God with every part of his life. He has given me a gift for which I owe his so much—passion for life. Thank you, T. —Laurie Daigle

To Terry:

The Little Seed

A mighty wind blew, and down came a seed.
"What" said a nearby flower, what do you need?
"Oh nothing" said the seed, just somewhere to grow.
You, see, I'm going to be a rose, or a tall tree, something great, that I know."
So patiently waited the seed through the sun and the rain.
What would he grow up to be? What would be his new name?
The seed knew he was special, it was just a matter of time.
One day he would wake up and oh, what he would find.
Well, it was almost overnight, the seed started to change.
He felt himself growing, it all seemed so strange.
He waited until daylight, "Oh, what a day this will be.
Will I be a beautiful flower or a big strong tree?"
The sun peeked out from the hills, and the seed was finally above ground.
The once excited seed was weary at what he found.
He had grown into a weed, only a bit higher than the dirt.
The little weed was disappointed, the little weed was hurt.
"God, why am I a weed, why would you set this path?
I provide no shade, or smell nice, and I'm only a little taller than the grass.
What could I possible accomplish that compares of a mighty tree?
Who's going to stop and look, who would ever want me?"
God looked at the little seed, and a smile grew on his face.
"I made everything with great thought, and I carefully put it in its place.
You, little seed, are in the perfect place. I know where I can find you, I created your sweet face.
I made you close to the ground, as you can probably see
I made you to blend in, your future is with me.

I made you with great thought in mind, that you wouldn't be here to stay.
No one will bother you, they won't take you away.
So you see little seed, you turned out just right.
I will never let you die. You will always be in my light."

Love,
Kaylan

Acknowledgements

I would like to express a very special thank you to the Baton Rouge Police Department for its tremendous support throughout this time. I want to especially thank Chief LeDuff for sharing our tears, as well as the great stories of everyday life as a cop. Chief LeDuff, words will never express our appreciation for your caring support.

Thank you Lieutenant Larry Hayes and the men in the narcotics division. These well-trained men are in harm's way every day. It helps to know that Terry worked with the best. All of the men in his unit worked hard, had fun and enjoyed what they did. Be safe, and thank you for your sacrifice.

To Susan D. Mustafa, my editor and collaborator on this book. I hope you know that God put you in my path to help me accomplish this project. When my thoughts and emotions were spinning out of control, you calmed me down, pointed me in the right direction and gently pushed me forward. Thank you.

To the incredible people of the city of Baton Rouge. Terry's death showed us that there are truly good people in the world. The support and the empathy that was shown was the source of strength for our family.

You will never know how much we will always cherish the outpouring of sympathy from our friends and family and this community.

Thank you to Frankie Caruso for loving Terry. We will only heal when we realize that God was in control, that there was nothing anyone could have done. Terry's day was written in God's book long before he was born. His purpose here was fulfilled, and he is still touching people's lives. I pray that God clouds what happened from your mind and allows you to be truly happy. Terry would want it.

Thanks to the Healing Place Church for helping us get through this difficult time. Your Christ-like service has reached so many people. Thank you Pastor Dino Rizzo for the most incredible service of the celebration of Terry's life. It touched so many people. But most of all, thank you for the dedication of the Terry Melancon Chapel in Mozambique, Africa. A protion of the proceeds from this book will be sent to help the church reach this immensely impoverished country.

To Lynn—Thank you for loving Terry so much. I know why he loved you, and we will always have a place in our family for you. Thank you for being you. You are my daughter-in-law, and I love you. *T, I'm taking care of her for you!*

And to my family—Lacey and Craig, Grace and Amelia, Kaylan and my husband, Terry—thank you so much. You are my life. I love all of you, and I am so grateful for your love and support. We are missing a chain in our family's link. Perhaps the chain will be linked back together for eternity when one by one we get to see our precious son and brother, Terry, once again.

Made in United States
North Haven, CT
23 February 2024

49062390R00104